A COMPANION GUIDE TO THE ROYAL CASTLE IN WARSAW

Jerzy Lileyko

A COMPANION GUIDE TO THE ROYAL CASTLE IN WARSAW

Translated by David Evans

Interpress Publishers, Warsaw 1980

ISBN-83-223-1935-5

TABLE OF CONTENTS

PART I
THE CASTLE AS A FORMER ROYAL RESIDENCE AND THE SEAT OF THE STATE AUTHORITY

PART II
THE HISTORY OF THE CASTLE

PART III
THE CASTLE REBUILT

PART IV
THE FORMER CASTLE COLLECTIONS
AND RECENT DONATIONS

PART I

THE CASTLE
AS A FORMER ROYAL
RESIDENCE AND THE SEAT
OF THE STATE AUTHORITY

THE COMMONWEALTH
OF THE TWO NATIONS

The Castle in Warsaw was once not only a royal residence but also the seat of the highest state authority as represented by the Seym (national parliament) and many supreme crown offices. To understand the role and function of the Royal Castle in the past it is necessary to recall the basis of the political system of old Poland, which began to take shape during the late Middle Ages and reached its final form in the middle of the 16th century. In 1569 at a meeting of the Polish and Lithuanian gentry at Lublin, which has gone down in history as the diet of the Union of Lublin, it was decided to unite the Kingdom of Poland and the Grand Duchy of Lithuania into one state. From that time on there was to be one Seym and Warsaw was chosen for its seat. The first Polish-Lithuanian joint Seym was in session at the Warsaw Castle from April to July 1570. The choice of Warsaw, centrally situated in the extensive state of the Jagiellonian kings, as the seat of the Seym resulted in frequent visits by king and court to the city and finally the royal residence was transferred here permanently. Officially, however, Cracow remained the capital of the Kingdom of Poland and Vilna that of the Grand Duchy of Lithuania.

After the death of the last king of the Jagiellonian dynasty, Sigismund Augustus, in 1572, Poland became an elective monarchy and all legislative power was vested in the Seym. The hereditary aspect of the monarchy was abandoned for ever and each king was to be elected by all the gentry. All dynastic aspirations by successive rulers until the end of the 18th century were fiercely opposed by the Seym and the political writers of that time and were seen as an attack on the system of government and rights of the gentry. Whereas in other European countries at that time absolute monarchies appeared, in Poland a state arose with republican characteristics of government with an elected king and a parliament having the sole right to promulgate laws. The basis of this system of government was the so-called "gentry democracy" which resulted from the deeply rooted myth of the equality of the entire gentry, an equality which could only be differentiated by the holding of state offices and church positions, obtained, at least in theory, for personal services and not arising out of rank of birth. An expression of the struggle to maintain equality for the entire gentry were the parliamentary decrees which banned the use and assumption of aristocratic titles. Socially the same phenomenon was found in the method of address which was generally used among the gentry of "my lord brother" and even the king used the same term when addressing them. They referred to themselves as "knights", a long-standing title derived from the distant past when each nobleman was to defend the state. It was just this tradition which was the source of the zealously cherished conviction of the equality of the entire estate of knights.

Under the influence of the widespread ideas of humanism and the revived interest in the classical world during the Renaissance, the previous Jagiellonian State had adopted the name of *Res Publica,* which then became *Rzeczpospolita Obojga Narodów* in Polish or the Commonwealth of the Two Nations. Contemporary writers and historians often drew a parallel between the ancient Roman Republic and Poland during the Renaissance period. This was most clearly expressed by the Chancellor Jan Zamoyski in his work *De Senatu romano* (1563) and in his speech of welcome to Henry of Valois who was chosen as the first elected king, when he called the magnates senators, the gentry patricians, the peasants Roman slaves, and deputies to the Seym tribunes of the people. Contemporary Poles felt that the Polish-Lithuanian Commonwealth attained a constitutional model which approximated to the kind represented by the

Principate of Augustus who governed together with his council as *primus inter pares*. In the Polish interpretation the council was represented by the Seym and Senate and the Polish king was very often designated as "first in council". The only states possessing this form of government at this time were Poland and Venice. Both the King of Poland and the Doge of Venice were elected by free citizens and governed with the help of a council while observing laws which provided the basis of permanence for both "republics".

The Commonwealth of the Two Nations was therefore a republic created by and for the gentry. In Poland, however, this estate was very numerous although clearly differentiated both materially and culturally. In the 18th century the gentry formed 10 per cent of the entire population of the country whereas in France, for example, they only constituted one per cent. Relatively broad and varied groups of society derived advantage from the privileges of gentry democracy and the myth of knighthood equality, and this created a specific attitude and social climate as reflected in political life, culture and art.

THE SEYM

The Warsaw Castle was the seat of the Seym and in a state with a parliamentary government this fact had considerable importance. The Parliament of the early Commonwealth consisted of three estates: the king, the senate, and the knights or delegates of local diets. The king was chosen by the gentry in free election, the senators were appointed by the king, and the deputies were elected by the gentry at local diets. The Senate and Seym deputies carried on their debates in separate rooms called chambers. In the Senatorial Chamber the king presided "sitting in state", i.e. on his throne under a canopy, while debates in the Chamber of Deputies were chaired by a Speaker elected by the deputies. To pass valid laws deputies went from the Chamber of Deputies to the Senatorial Chamber, which procedure was called "the union of the estates". Only all three estates — king, senate, and deputies — in joint session could pass a bill which became law.

In the Chamber of Deputies the deputies sat on benches covered with red cloth and only the Speaker sat on a chair although it had to have a low back and be on the same level as the deputies' benches. This minor detail was to illustrate the principle of equality of the knights' estate. The Speaker's chair was called the *locus directoralis*. During the 16th and most of the 17th century the manner of arranging the benches and the Speaker's chair was adapted to the architectural form of an extended Chamber of Deputies. In the second half of the 18th century the shape was changed to that of a rectangle — almost a square — and the benches were arranged in a semi-circle on both sides opposite the Speaker's chair in such a way that the centre of the hall was left empty. In the rear behind the Speaker's chair there was a slightly raised seat surrounded by a railing where there was a table at which sat the Secretary of the Seym and those appointed to write down laws and statutes.

The central place in the Senatorial Chamber was the royal throne, i.e. a sumptuous chair with a high back placed on a level several steps higher and with a canopy over it. On the right and left hand side of the throne the senatorial seats were placed in two rows the length of the room. The most important seat — on the right of the throne — was occupied by the Archbishop of Gniezno, the Primate of Poland. His seat had a slightly higher back than those of the other senators. During the sessions of the Senate a canon held a tall cross — the symbol of the dignity of the primate — behind the archbishop's chair. On the left of the throne sat the Archbishop of Lvov. Next came the seats of the bishops, the mayors, and the castellans, first the so-called chief ones, then the lesser ones.

Opposite the throne on the shorter side of the room, seats were arranged for ministers — Polish on the right, Lithuanian on the left. Grand marshals, chancellors, chancellery and treasury officials, and court marshals of the two nations were numbered among the category of ministers. When a "union of the estates" took place, the regional deputies stood behind the senatorial seats. Only the Speaker (Marshal) of the Chamber of Deputies sat with the ministers. His seat was opposite the royal throne between the chairs of the Grand Marshal of Poland and the Grand Marshal of Lithuania, but it had a lower back than the ministerial chairs. One of the deputies held a staff behind the Speaker's chair as a symbol of marshal dignity.

The head of state during interregna was the Primate of Poland. During the sessions of the Senate and the Convocation and Electoral Seyms, he presided in Senate as the interrex. His seat was placed in front of the canopy at the foot of the royal throne.

Immediately after the Union of Lublin the Senate consisted of 142 senators and the Chamber of Deputies of 170 deputies. During the 17th century the number of deputies increased a little while the order of seating in the Senate was determined by the shape of the room in the form of an extended rectangle, which apart from the throne had to accommodate 142 senatorial chairs and all the regional deputies. The Senatorial Chamber was extended several times but always retained its rectangular shape and the arrangement of the throne and the senatorial and ministerial chairs. In the Chamber of Deputies there were benches for about 170 deputies and some extra space where the arbitrators sat. Both parliamentary chambers were extremely large.

Each session of the Seym began with a service in St. John's Church during which the court chaplain gave the sermon usually devoted to the subject of the debates-to-come. Among contemporaries the most highly regarded parliamentary sermons were those of Piotr Skarga in which he reprimanded the selfish magnates and gentry and urged them to rectify the constitution of the Commonwealth. It was this very scene of the inspired preacher giving a sermon before the session of the Seym in front of King Sigismund III, the senators, and deputies that Jan Matejko painted in 1864. After the service the deputies accompanied the king and senators to the Senatorial Chamber and then returned to the Chamber of Deputies. The Speaker of the previous parliamentary session, called "the old staff", opened the debates and arranged the election of a new Speaker. After the election had been completed and a majority of votes given, the Speaker "of the old staff" read out the words of oath which the newly elected Speaker repeated: "I swear by Almighty God that I shall not accept, sign, or inscribe *in volumen legum* [in the statute book] any law which was not passed unanimously... I shall have allegiance to no man, only to the Commonwealth itself as assembled in the Seym." Then the former Speaker handed his successor a staff as a symbol of office.

After the opening of the new session in the Chamber of Deputies, the deputies went to the Senate to greet the king. The progress of the procession of deputies with the Speaker at their head, in front of whom one of the deputies carried a raised staff, was of a particularly solemn nature. In the Senatorial Chamber the Grand Marshal welcomed the deputies and then the Speaker and Chancellor delivered speeches. After the introductory speeches the deputies went one by one to the throne and kissed the king's hand. Now the ceremonial part of the opening of the parliamentary session was over and the Seym proceeded to its debates.

The etiquette for parliamentary debates and in particular the custom for the deputies to proceed to the Senatorial Chamber required ample passageways and appropriately designed large accommodation. The arrangement of the rooms which was put into effect directly after the Union of Lublin by Giovanni Battista Quadro between 1570 and 1572 and converted and improved several times in the 17th and 18th centuries completely satisfied these requirements. Thus as early the second half of the 16th century there was a building in the Warsaw Castle which was intended exclusively for parliamentary affairs and adapted to the ceremonial of the Seym.

THE KING

After the Jagiellonian dynasty died out, each king of Poland was chosen by free election which usually took place in the open air in the village of Wielka Wola not far from Warsaw. Every member of the gentry could take part in the royal election and thus these assemblies were extraordinarily large. For the election of Ladislaus IV in 1632 around 70,000 gentry journeyed to Warsaw. Francis Gordon, an observer from the English court who was present in Warsaw at that time, wrote: "Never in my life have I seen anything like this and I don't know whether I'll see anything like it again."

Sometimes the elections made only stormy progress and resulted in rioting or the election of two candidates. In principle the legal winner was the candidate whose election was announced by the Primate. Directly after the election, the king-elect pledged to observe the so-called Henrician Articles which had been passed in 1573 for Henry of Valois, the first king chosen by free election, and were also binding for his successors. This usually took place in St. John's Church. The Articles were a collection of principles defining the scope of royal power and authority. In addition, at each Electoral Seym, the gentry passed other resolutions, called the *pacta conventa,* the contents of which varied depending on who had been elected king. Whereas in other countries the will or whim of the king was law, in Poland every king-elect had to make the following oath before his coronation: "If We do anything against the laws, rights, and articles, which God forbid, We free Our citizens of both nations from the obedience and loyalty which is due to Us."

Royal authority was therefore closely restricted by the law but it still covered a rather wide area. The king appointed all mayors, castellans and ministers and had direct influence on the appointment of bishops. Also the distribution of ecclesiastical benefits and landed estates (the so-called starosties) was part of the king's sphere of authority. No parliamentary bill could be passed without the approval of the king.

A consequence of the republican constitution of the Commonwealth was the separation of royal income from state income. A decree on this matter was passed by the Seym in 1590. Funds for the upkeep of the court came from the Wieliczka saltmines, Polish and Lithuanian customs levies and large landed estates known as the *ekonomia.* Income raised from these sources constituted the material basis for royal patronage and court artistic enterprises. The king did not levy taxes for his own needs. If the Seym approved tax levies, these were earmarked for public matters, most frequently for army recruitment or national defences. The royal income and treasury were administered by the Court Treasurer and the state finances by the Royal Grand Treasurer who was responsible for income and expenditure only to the Seym. Therefore the ever-changing adornments of the royal apartments and the art collections assembled by monarchs were regarded as the private property of the royal family. Thus in Poland conditions never existed to create royal art collections whose continuation was assured by an hereditary dynasty as in other European countries and which eventually passed into public museums. The only items regarded as national property were the jewel collection in the royal treasury and the collection of tapestries commissioned in the middle of the 16th century by King Sigismund Augustus in Flanders and bequeathed by the king to the Commonwealth in his will. These tapestries decorated the rooms of the Cracow and Warsaw Castles during various national celebrations. They were last used to adorn the apartments of the Warsaw Castle for the coronation ceremony of Stanislaus Augustus in 1764.

The kings of Poland chosen by free election did not become hereditary owners but only life-long tenants of the residences in the two capitals of Cracow and Vilna, as well as the castle in the parliamentary seat of Warsaw. The official landlord of the Castle was the *Starosta* (Governor) of Warsaw and during the interregnum it was available for the use of the Archbishop of Gniezno, the Primate of Poland; order and security within the Castle walls was the responsibility of the Royal Grand Marshal and state property assembled here was looked after by the Royal Treasurer. This gave the Warsaw Castle a character completely different from other royal residences in Europe where generally the property of the dynasty was identified with the property of the state. In the Warsaw Castle the king was only the tenant of certain apartments called the royal rooms. The rest of the large building was occupied by rooms for the Seym, offices, archives, and courtrooms.

THE FIRST BUILDING
IN THE COMMONWEALTH

In the minds of the gentry the Warsaw Castle was not one of the many residences of the elected monarch but the seat of the Seym of the Commonwealth of the Two Nations where the king was but one of the estates. Its official title was also an expression of this point of view. In parliamentary statutes, inventories, treasury accounts and other documents the Castle was preceded by the word "Warsaw" or called "the Castle of His Royal Majesty and the Commonwealth". This title was highly important as it reflected the actual form of the socio-political system in Poland at that time.

The similar political system of Venice and Poland was also shown in the similarity of the Doge's Palace and the Warsaw Royal Castle; not an architectural similarity but a functional similarity as fulfilled by the two buildings. This analogy was also clear to contemporaries. In his *Memoires... contenant ses divers voyages en Pologne,* published in 1698 in Paris under the pseudonym of Chevalier de Beaujeu, the French traveller Francois Paulin d'Aleyrac noted that the Warsaw Castle "is in reality the palace of a republic inhabited by kings where there is one room for the senate and one for the gentry who meet there during parliamentary sessions. Council meetings, ambassadorial interviews, and courts take place there like in Venice where the Doge is accommodated in the palace of the government as the head of the Republic". The peculiar fact that the royal residence was the property of the state also caught the attention of other foreigners and this was explicitly mentioned by Louis de Jaucourt in the 17th volume of Diderot's *Grande Encyclopédie*, published in 1765.

The many offices also gave the royal residence the aspect of a public building. The royal chancellery was housed here, administered by the Royal Grand Chancellor and deputy chancellor, documents were drafted, written, and given the official seal, and copies of them were entered into the chancellery book or the Royal Register. These registers were kept in a separate archive. The court treasury department and the Marshal's office were also in the Castle. Various courts sat there including parliamentary courts passing judgment on high treason, courts for the feifdoms of Ducal Prussia and Courland, presided over by the king, and the secret tribunals during the interregnum. In addition the Warsaw court of the first instance had its headquarters here as did the municipal chancellery, court of law, and archive. All this activity required a certain number of staff permanently employed since crowds of petitioners passed through official chambers. When the Seym was in session, the public always came to hear the debates in the Chamber of Deputies.

Thus everyone, apart from the common people, had the right of entry to the Castle, the offices inside it, and the parliamentary rooms. From many years before the custom had existed in Poland of the right of every member of the gentry, not only dignitaries and courtiers, to be able to enter the royal apartments. This right was only restricted to the extent necessary to guarantee the king's safety and rest. It should be emphasized that, apart from one incident in 1620 when Piekarski, an insane nobleman, attacked Sigismund III with an ice-pick, no attempt was ever made on the king's life in spite of the fact that in Poland access to the king was exceptionally easy.

The greater use of the Castle for official rather than residential functions was one of the reasons for the elected kings building their own private palaces in the Warsaw suburbs. The kings of the Vasa dynasty built Ujazdów Castle and Kazimierzowski Palace, called the Villa Regia in the 17th century (it is now the main building of Warsaw University). Both of these residences were surrounded by extensive gardens and looked like Italian suburban villas. Beautiful Wilanów Palace was built for John III Sobieski. King Stanislaus Leszczyński had his family residence in Leszno (no longer in existence) and the kings of the Saxon Wettin line had the Saxon Palace (burnt down in 1944). And it is to Stanislaus Augustus Poniatowski that Warsaw owes the architectural gem of Łazienki Palace.

The variety of functions fulfilled by the Warsaw Castle influenced its architectural shape, especially in the planning of the area occupied by the royal apartments, the

Seym, and the crown offices. The royal apartments had to be adapted to the etiquette and customs of the court and the headquarters of the various offices to the accepted method of administration of that period. The organizational structure of the Seym and the parliamentary procedure imposed an architectural framework on the parliamentary building.

The king resided at the Castle, but the upkeep of the building was the responsibility of the Commonwealth Treasury. The Seym and the Senate Council often interfered in matters to do with building, undertaking decisions to extend or redecorate the Castle, and assigning specific expenses for this purpose. The reason for this interference was often political and only appeared to be concerned with the artistic intentions of the king. When Augustus II planned to undertake a splendid renovation of the royal throne in 1721 the deputies and Senate did not concur, using the argument that this would result in the excessive elevation of the person of the monarch which could warrant his absolutist and dynastic aspirations which were generally known. The Polish gentry and their representatives in the Seym were exceptionally sensitive to this kind of apparent trifle. It has to be admitted, however, that if the king's artistic enterprises in the Castle were in agreement with the national administration, they won universal approval. This is how it happened when the Chamber of Deputies and the Senatorial Chamber were decorated with symbolic scenes portraying the apotheosis of the Commonwealth on the instigation of John III and when Stanislaus Augustus put into effect ambitious plans to decorate the royal apartments in a pointedly nationalistic style to show Poland's past.

From the close of the 16th century on, the gentry increasingly restricted royal authority in the spheres of governmental, financial, and military affairs. Gradually the centre of administration was concentrated in the Seym. Also at this period the idea that the Seym was a body with sovereign power in the state first came into being. In parliamentary pronouncements at this time the Chamber of Deputies was often called the Temple of Laws, an expression which, in spite of its baroque rhetoric, doubtlessly stated the general point of view.

In a letter to the Treasurer Karol Siedlnicki written in 1751, the Royal Grand Marshal Franciszek Bieliński said that the Castle was "the allotted Residence of the Monarchs, the *conclave consiliorum,* and the *Officina Regum*". The conviction which the gentry felt, that the system of government of the Commonwealth had all the characteristics of a perfect system, resulted in them turning a secular building into a shrine, and this particular fact has to be recognized as something which distinguished the Castle from all other European residences.

In the minds of contemporaries neither the age-old Wawel Castle in Cracow nor any other royal residence apart from the Castle in "the residential city of His Royal Majesty" of Warsaw was the "principal" building in the state, the *conclave consiliorum,* personifying the majesty of the Commonwealth. This was the reason why the Seym paid attention to its upkeep, beautification and renovation, this was the reason for interference by deputies and the Council of the Senate in royal plans for works of art which ran contrary to the concept of the Commonwealth established since the time of the Union of Lublin, and finally this was the reason for the building designs of those kings to whom the majesty of the state was not a trivial matter, e.g. John III and Stanislaus Augustus.

THE CASTLE AS THE SYMBOL OF POLISH SOVEREIGNTY

During the period of the partition of the territory of the former Polish-Lithuanian Commonwealth, a temporary Polish state arose as a result of the Napoleonic Wars called the Duchy of Warsaw (1807—15). After the fall of Napoleon, the Congress of Vienna called into being the Kingdom of Poland (1815—31) with its own constitution, Seym, and army, but linked by personal union with Russia, the Russian tsar being simultaneously king of Poland.

In spite of the changes in the whole framework of Polish nationhood, the Warsaw Castle remained as before the residence of the monarch and the seat of the Seym. However this function was simply a tradition without the ideological basis of former times. A king was imposed on the country by a foreign power and the role of the Seym was trivial or simply decorative.

However, under the influence of the ideals of Romanticism, which were particularly strong in Polish cultural life, the Castle began to take on a new role in the consciousness of the people and was linked with the national struggle for independence. During the November Uprising of 1830-1, the Revolutionary Seym of the Kingdom of Poland in the course of its debates which were full of patriotic fervour dethroned the tsar as the king of Poland.

This decision by the Seym became the reason — after the collapse of the uprising — for the deliberate and systematic dismantling of the Castle, when the rooms for the Seym were destroyed and all pictures, sculptures, and decorations illustrating the sovereignty of Poland were exported or removed. Thus the Castle shared the fate of a subject nation. During the January Uprising in 1863, Castle Square became the scene of demonstrations by the population of Warsaw which were bloodily suppressed. The memory of these events was kept alive by dozens of drawings, sketches, and pictures. Illustrations of the events in Castle Square appeared in numerous European magazines at that time. No motif became as popular in Polish art in the 19th century as the Column of Sigismund III against the sky with the flat façade of the Castle with its slender tower and a swirling crowd of demonstrators in the background. People demonstrated in front of the Castle because they remembered that the building was once the seat of government of an independent Poland. They were reminded of this by the tin banderole with the golden eagle on top of the spire crowning the cupola of the Sigismund Tower. The Castle began to acquire a symbolic meaning, recalling the inalienable right of the Poles to determine their own fate. This idea was popularized through wide sections of society by poetry (Cyprian Kamil Norwid) and art (Artur Grottger), and the great visionary of Poland's past, Jan Matejko, bequeathed to the nation his great work painted in 1891, "The Third of May Constitution", with the hope that it would adorn the chamber of the Seym in the Warsaw Castle in an independent Poland. For indeed no one doubted that one day the building would regain its former splendour. When on 11 November 1918 an independent Poland became a fact, on the same day red-and-white flags were unfurled on the towers of the Castle as if to sanctify this great and long-awaited moment.

However the Castle did not regain its traditional functions as the seat of the head of state and parliament in the reborn Polish state. The first legislative Seym was assembled in a building adapted to this purpose in Wiejska Street. In 1926 the Royal Castle became the residence of the President of the Republic and many state ceremonies and official receptions took place in the castle rooms, which were widely publicized by photo-reports in illustrated magazines and film newsreels.

The Castle came to be fixed in the national consciousness as a building in which the sovereignty of the Polish state was demonstrated. Once again it became the first building of a reborn Poland. The carefully restored elevations and interiors and also the artistic collections assembled here showed Poles and foreigners Polish culture and its place among the countries of Europe.

Traditions dating from the distant times of the Gentry Commonwealth, the romantic image of the Castle created in the period of partition when it served as a background for many incidents in the struggle for independence, and also the role of the Castle in reborn Poland had a symbolic significance in the mind of every Pole. This was the very reason why Hitler with his insane obsession with destroying entire nations and their cultures took the decision to blow up the building. However the Poles saved every work of art, every piece of decoration from the Castle since all of these remains were the material elements of an ideological symbol. The soldiers of the Polish Army who liberated the ruins of Warsaw on 17 January 1945 set up a guard of honour in front of the fallen figure of King Sigismund III. The idea of paying military honours to a king in People's Poland was only an apparent paradox. For ultimately this symbolic meaning of the Castle for all Poles was the basis for the decision to rebuild it.

In conclusion, let us quote the words of Henryk Jabłoński, the President of the Council of State of the

Polish People's Republic, at a meeting of the Citizens' Committee for the Rebuilding of the Royal Castle in Warsaw, who said: "The Warsaw Castle was the witness of innumerable events, days of glory and days of defeat, and when the Poles were a subject nation, it reminded people by its very existence of the fact that Warsaw was a capital and that its changing and stormy fortunes were intimately connected with the fortunes of the nation. And of course it was bound to acquire a particular meaning, full of symbolic content, in the hearts and minds of all Poles. The era of People's Poland has not removed this but has given new substance to it, immeasurably important for the future developments in our country. This has been shown in the great task of rebuilding Warsaw."

PART II

THE HISTORY
OF THE CASTLE

THE MIDDLE AGES

At the turn of the 13th and 14th centuries in the place where the Castle now stands a small fortified settlement made of wood and earth was built, probably originating as the residence of a local duke. Mazovia (the part of Poland where Warsaw is situated) was at that time a region linked to the Polish crown only as a feifdom. A minor branch of the Piast dynasty ruled here, descended from the offsprings of Boleslaus the Curly. When in 1320 Ladislaus the Short united the fragmented Piast principalities and was crowned in Cracow as king of Poland, Mazovia was not included in the territory of united Poland.

It is not yet clear whether the city of Warsaw, founded on a regular geometric plan on the lines of standard medieval town planning, was built at the same time as the castellum or whether the castellum was built a few decades earlier. Professor Aleksander Gieysztor, the famous expert on the Middle Ages, links the foundation of the castellum and city with the person of Duke Boleslaus II (1251—1313). We also know that the city and castellum were joined by a common defence system, first by an earth rampart and later by a brick wall.

The first written reference to Warsaw dates from 1311. In 1339, when the city was already fortified and wealthy, action was brought before the papal court here by the Polish King Casimir the Great against the German order of the Knights of St. Mary the Virgin known as the Teutonic Knights. The reason for this extraordinary action was the annexation of the Polish territories of Pomerania and Kuyavia by the Knights. Pope Benedict XII sent his judges from Avignon for the trial. The verdict in favour of Poland recognizing the total guilt of the Knights in the case was announced in St. John's Church which still exists today. In the records of the trial it is also written that the son of Boleslaus II, Duke Trojden (1284—1341), had his permanent residence and held his courts in Warsaw and was thus characterized by the papal diplomats: "This very duke cherishes peace for all inhabitants and visitors, dispenses justice, and allows no one in his realm to be unjustly oppressed."

Trojden's successor was Ziemowit (III) the Old. Trojden's and Ziemowit's residence was probably still made of wood. The first brick building on the site of the duke's castle, the high Grodzka (Town) Tower, also called the Large Tower, was built around the middle of the 14th century. In the Middle Ages the tower was a free-standing construction. On its north side was an annexe in which there was a well. As early as the 15th century the tower had partly collapsed and contemporary documents refer to it as *Turris Fracta,* i.e. the broken tower. It has been preserved in its medieval form today only up to the height of the first storey. The cellar of the Grodzka Tower contained a prison for the gentry. Coats-of-arms, signs, and inscriptions carved in the walls by prisoners can still be seen today.

It is possible that there were two fortified residential complexes on the site of the present Castle as early as the 14th century. One situated near St. John's Church was called *Curia Minor,* i.e. the small court, in 15th century documents, and the other, near the Castle Tower, was called *Curia Maior,* i.e. the large court. On the instigation of Duke Janusz (I) the Old (d. 1429) several brick buildings were erected on the latter site, of which the so-called Large House, a monumental Gothic building assigned as the ducal residence, was preserved until 1944. Of the interior only a large room with intersecting vaulting supported on one pillar has survived. The other Gothic buildings were either destroyed in the course of subsequent Castle improvements or absorbed by the new Castle and today only a few remains of them are known.

After the death of the last Mazovian Piasts — Stanislaus

I (d. 1524) and Janusz III (d. 1526) — Mazovia was incorporated within the Polish kingdom, and Warsaw, after being the capital of a separate principality, became one of the provincial towns in the state. However Princess Anna, the sister of the last Mazovian dukes, continued to reside in the Castle for several more years. In 1536 she took as her husband Stanisław Odrowąż, a Podolyan voivode, and departed for her husband's property in Podolye, thus severing finally the links between Warsaw and the royal Piast dynasty which had lasted for several centuries. It was probably her idea to have a group picture painted of the last rulers of Mazovia, Stanislaus I, Janusz III, and Anna, by which the last of the Piast line wished to commemorate a vanished dynasty. This portrait was bequeathed to the Warsaw Town Hall where it remained until the beginning of the 20th century. Now part of the Castle Collection, it is evidence of its lengthy Piast tradition.

THE CASTLE
UNDER THE JAGIELLONIANS

The royal residence

After settling down in Warsaw the Polish kings of the Jagiellonian dynasty frequently undertook building and decorating work on the Castle. It was not, however, very extensive and did not influence the architectural form of the building in any fundamental way. After the death of Sigismund (I) the Old in 1548 Mazovia was handed over to Queen Bona as her widow's settlement. Bona, who was from the Italian Sforza d'Aragon family and the daughter of Duke Gian Galeazzo Sforza of Milan and Isabella of Aragon, was one of the most illustrious women ever to sit on the throne of Poland. Her rule over Mazovia and Warsaw was memorable for her many economic initiatives which improved the productivity of the farms there. The widowed queen resided in the Gothic Castle of the Mazovian dukes and in Ujazdów, a village not far from Warsaw on the picturesque Vistula escarpment where she built a summer residence in the Italian style — a *villa suburbana* — surrounded by a large garden with regularly laid out flower beds and vegetation in geometrical shapes.

Caligari, the papal nuncio, who saw the Ujazdów residence in 1580, admired its beautiful situation over the Vistula and its Italian-style gardens and also liked "the palace which is completely made of wood, a local custom, but still beautiful".

Beneath the Warsaw Castle Queen Bona kept her legendary treasure. In 1556 as a result of a contretemps with her son, King Sigismund Augustus, the old queen decided to leave Poland and return to Italy to the family principality of Bari. It is written in the old chronicles that out of the castle gates came the royal carriage with 24 wagons, loaded with treasure and jewels and pulled by 144 horses.

The transformation of the Large House into the Seym building (1570—72)

Sigismund Augustus intended to rebuild the Warsaw Castle as early as 1563 and in that year the royal architects designed a model for a new castle. We do not know whether it was approved by the king or intended to be carried out. Construction finally began in the summer of 1569. At the same time the diet of the Polish and Lithuanian gentry took place in Lublin at which Warsaw was chosen as the place for their joint parliamentary debates and the Castle, the former seat of the Mazovian dukes, was assigned as the parliamentary building. With the decision of the Lublin diet, the rebuilding of the Warsaw Castle as a parliamentary building was immediately embarked upon.

Two famous architects of Italian ancestry who were active in Poland at that time — Giovanni Battista Quadro and Giacomo Pario — were engaged to carry out the rebuilding. Quadro had lived since 1550 in Poznań where he was the municipal architect and had designed the magnificent Renaissance town hall. Pario, whose name usually appears in the changed form of Pahr, had been in the service of the ducal court of the Legnica-Brzeg branch of the Piast line in Silesia. In Brzeg he had built a Renaissance palace with a cloistered courtyard, modelled on the courtyard of the Wawel royal castle. Although after signing the contract Pario left Warsaw and returned to Silesia, thus putting Quadro at risk, lest he have to return the payment which both architects had received together from the royal treasury, it can be assumed that the plans for the new castle were carried out jointly. Of the work that was carried out in Warsaw at that time, mention is due to the completely new building of the so-called New Royal House, which was intended as the king's residence and work on which was carried out between 1569 and 1572, and the rebuilding of the former Large House of the Mazovian dukes as the parliamentary building between 1570 and 1572.

The rebuilding of the Large House which was undertaken by Quadro changed the external appearance of the building to a small degree. The north and south elevations were surmounted by narrow late-Renaissance gables, the form of which was certainly similar to those planned earlier by Quadro for the Municipal Weight House in Poznań.

The west elevation was decorated with paintings in the form of the coats-of-arms of the state and the king as well as the provinces and regions making up the Polish-Lithuanian Commonwealth. The remains of these decorations were revealed between 1921 and 1924 from beneath layers of later plasterwork. They showed a Polish eagle interwoven with the monogram "SA" (Sigismundus Augustus) and two smaller shields, one with the Pogoń (Pursuit) coat-of-arms of the Jagiellonian dynasty, and the other with that of the Habsburgs which belonged to the third wife of Sigismund Augustus, Catherine of Mantua. This decoration, consisting of the coats-of-arms of the state, the ruler and the lands of the Commonwealth, clearly emphasized the ideological function of the building in which the Seym held its debates as the highest authority in the Commonwealth together with the king.

The interior of the Large House underwent a considerably greater transformation. A large hall was constructed on the ground floor which was over 30 m long and 10 m wide and designed for the deputies debates. A row of six pillars which supported the vaulting divided the hall into two parts. This architectural format conformed to the role of the interior as a place for public debates. In the one part the debates took place and in the other the public gathered to observe them. Near the Chamber of Deputies was a square-shaped room with vaulting supported on one pillar, which was used as the Seym chancellery. The Grodzka Tower and the annexe which was linked to the Large House on the south side held flight of steps. Upstairs was the Senatorial Vestibule from which wide doors led to the Senatorial Chamber. There, directly opposite the entrance, stood the royal throne and on either side of the throne along the hall were two rows of seats for the senators. During the joint debates in the Senatorial Chamber the deputies stood behind the senators' chairs. The room had a coffered ceiling, decorated with gilded rosettes, and during parliamentary sessions expensive Flemish tapestries were hung on the walls which were a favourite type of decoration for public and private rooms in Poland in the 16th century. The Senatorial Chamber adjoined a large square-shaped room called the Large Hall. This room linked the private apartments of the king with the parliamentary rooms.

The royal apartments were in the New Royal House which was situated at a 120° angle in relation to the Large House. This irregular siting of the two buildings was due to the layout of the edge of the Vistula escarpment. A round tower containing a flight of stairs was erected where the Large House and the New Royal House met. The stairs led to the aforementioned Great Hall and from there to the royal apartments. The New Royal House was absorbed in the later Baroque castle and at the beginning of the 17th century was completely rebuilt. We do not know what its original Renaissance architectural form was like as none of the plans have been preserved and the bills for construction from 1569—72 do not permit us to make too many hypotheses. However, the New Royal House was certainly a smallish building intended only as a temporary residence for the king during the parliamentary session. We do not know either whether it was the intention of Sigismund Augustus only to transform the Large House into the parliamentary building and build a small residence nearby or whether these plans were just the first stage of some larger venture.

At the same time a second residential complex in the Warsaw Castle, in the Middle Ages known as the *Curia*

Minor, where Sigismund Augustus' sister, Princess Anna the Jagiellonian lived, was also rebuilt. The original form of these buildings, too, was lost during the course of the following centuries.

The rebuilding work on the Castle was stopped in 1572 in connection with the unexpected death of Sigismund Augustus. Not much of what had been done by then apart from the arrangement of the parliamentary rooms has survived till the present time. However, the rebuilding under the Jagiellonians deserves our attention as for the first time in Poland, and doubtless in Europe too, an attempt had been made to construct a building which was intended exclusively for parliamentary use. Quadro and Pario fulfilled their contract so well that their arrangement of the parliamentary rooms remained unchanged until the last quarter of the 17th century.

The employment of these two architects whose work, preserved until today, bears witness to their capabilities, makes us assume that the rebuilding of the Castle which was in their charge was intended to create a splendid work of architecture. However, some disputes, certainly of an artistic nature, arose between the king and his architects. Sigismund Augustus, art patron and connoisseur, wrote in a letter in 1571, that "the buildings which these bricklayers have started on pleases Us not one bit".

After the death of Sigismund Augustus the Seyms assembled at the Warsaw Castle. Queen Anna the Jagiellonian and her husband, Stephen Báthory, the second king of Poland to be chosen by free election, also resided here. At this time no major plans for construction were carried out. The great rebuilding of the Castle did not begin until the reign of Sigismund III of the House of Vasa.

THE CASTLE DURING
THE VASA PERIOD

The work undertaken between 1598 and 1619

Warsaw had been the seat of the Seym since 1569. On average the Polish Seym assembled here every two years, sometimes annually, and even more often than that.

During the period of the parliamentary session the king had to be present in Warsaw. Therefore the royal court had to make constant journeys between the capital, Cracow, and the parliamentary seat, Warsaw. In addition Sigismund III had inherited the throne of Sweden in succession to his father John III and Warsaw was closer to Sweden than Cracow. These considerations laid at the root of the decision by Sigismund III to transfer the royal residence permanently from Cracow to Warsaw. This process took place in stages and lasted about ten years beginning in 1597 when the royal family left Cracow after a fire in the Wawel.

However, the small Royal House of Sigismund Augustus at the Warsaw Castle was not suitable for a permanant residence for the king, his family, his court, and the many crown departments. Thus the decision was taken to build a new large residence. The designer was the court architect Giovanni Trevano. Polish art historians have long studied the matter whether the Venetian Vincenzo Scamozzi, one of the most famous Italian Renaissance architects, took part in the construction of the new Warsaw castle. We know that he was in contact with Poles and did various commissions for Polish customers. At the time when the plans for the Warsaw Castle were being drawn up he was twice in Poland, once in 1592 in the suite of the Venetian envoy, Pietro Duodo, and again in 1598. It seems probable that King Sigismund III, who was captivated by Italian art and Venetian art in particular, showed or submitted the construction plans he intended to use in Warsaw to the illustrious Venetian for examination. This seems likely, but so far this attractive assumption has not yet been authoritatively confirmed.

The new Castle was built on a pentagonal plan with a large inner grand courtyard. The buildings on the edge of the escarpment, which up to then had been freestanding, the Gothic Large House and the Royal House, were substantially enlarged and incorporated as southeast and north-east wings into the compact block of the pentagonal building. Three new wings were begun from scratch — the north, the west with the high Royal or Sigismund Tower, and the south. Work on the building proceeded for almost twenty years. In the first stage

(1601—5) the Royal House was extended and the vaulting in the Deputies' Chamber was altered. The whole five-sided building was basically ready by 1611 and this was followed by finishing details over the next few years. In 1619 a copper cupola was added to the Royal Tower and this date is accepted as the final work on the building, although various items of construction went on for the next few years. After 1620, in connection with the threat of a Turkish invasion of Poland, the escarpment beneath the Castle was strengthened by a strong wall with two towers. These fortifications gave the new royal residence, when viewed from the Vistula side, the appearance of a modern *palazzo in forteza*. Further construction work, which was either a continuation or a completion of the fortification idea, was carried out under Ladislaus IV between 1637 and 1645.

The new castle was designed with a view to maintaining the principles of Baroque symmetry inasmuch as this was possible within the existing city and medieval defence walls. The facade of the newly-built west wing with its high tower in the middle and two turrets on the corners, faced the town and was very near to Przedzamkowa Street which ran along the present western side of Castle Square, from the Cracow Gate to the junction with Świętojańska Street which led to the Market Place. In front of the west wing and façade was the Front Courtyard (*avant cour*), where the low buildings of the stables, coach-houses, royal pharmacy, and kitchen were constructed. This courtyard had a triangular shape because of the town buildings which were already in existence and particularly because of Przedzamkowa Street which had been laid out as early as the Middle Ages and was the main thorough-fare between the Cracow Gate and the Market Place. However, the buildings of the Front Courtyard were shaped in such a way that its irregular design was rela-tively little noticed. Along Przedzamkowa Street was a gate through which the main route to the castle area passed, first to the Front Courtyard and then through the gate in the Royal or Sigismund Tower which was situated in a straight line, to the imposing, pentagonal Grand Courtyard. This axis was finished off by a tower, built in the reign of Sigismund Augustus and later called the

Ladislaus Tower, which contained the main staircase leading to the royal chambers. In the side wings there were two more gates — the Grodzka Gate in the south wing and the Senators' Gate in the north wing.

The low buildings on the Front Courtyard with their modest architectural design formed an important element in the composition of the entire Castle layout. The difficult task of creating a modern residence within the medieval structure of a town enclosed by fortifications, was solved by Trevano in a way not lacking in a certain picturesqueness. We must remember that the Castle was connected in its composition with the Old Town and not with Krakowskie Przedmieście which at the beginning of the 17th century was not yet the main street in Warsaw. As a result the façade was turned to Piwna and Świętojańska streets in the Old Town, which at that time were the main streets in the city. Within this spatial framework the architect made use of all possibilities to emphasize the dignity of the royal residence. The Royal Tower was so situated that it completed the viewing angle from Piwna and Świętojańska streets. At the beginning of Piwna Street was the Świętojańska Gate behind which the narrow tower loomed in the background. Therefore this solution had the appearance of an axial layout in accordance with the requirements of modern town planning.

Within the total plan of the castle buildings, which were linked as a composition with the town, the castle façade was supposed to act simply as a silhouette, looming over the neighbouring buildings. Hence certain characteristics arose which today are regarded as shortcomings, like its excessive horizontal length and its ground floor which is too low, which were glaringly disclosed after the Cracow Gate and the buildings on the Front Courtyard were burned down at the beginning of the 19th century and an irregular square was laid out in their place which is completely foreign to the original Baroque spatial plan.

The elevations of all the castle wings made use of an identical architectural decoration which was reminiscent of the stern forms of early Roman Baroque. The area of the elevations was not marked by any architectural divisions and their diversity had only been effected by harmoniously arranged windows in small, sectional frames. The elevations were also decorated with rustications in the corners and with gate portals.

It has to be admitted that the most interesting artistic work on the castle is the main west façade with its high tower facing the town. Its general architectural form, rusticated corners and portal, and strongly emphasized *piano nobile* show that the source of inspiration for the castle façade were the palaces in Rome designed by Carlo Maderno and Giacomo della Porta. However in relation to the original Roman models the façade of the Warsaw Castle was enriched by vertical elements in the shape of a central tower and two corner turrets.

The main façade of the Baroque royal residence was supposed to show the strength and majesty of government. This part was played by the palaces in Rome and the same function was bestowed on the castle façade, although emphasized in an even more clear way. Its powerful mass looming over the buildings of the town was the first achievement of this kind in Polish architecture. It linked together elements of Roman architecture with northern influences as shown by the high tower. In this connection it is easy to spot the complete originality of this building in which forms and ideas worked out under Italian skies were adapted to city requirements and imaginations or to "Polish skies and customs" as the anonymous author of a Polish article on architecture put it in 1659. This conceptual expression of the new royal residence was the work of Sigismund III, who at the beginning of his reign strove to limit parliamentary government in Poland, and to introduce hereditary succession and absolutist rule.

The parliamentary rooms

As a result of the expanding of the Castle described above the former Gothic Large House became incorporated as one of the wings of the new pentagonal design. The parliamentary rooms remained in the same place, the Chamber of Deputies on the ground floor and the Senatorial Chamber on the first floor. Between 1601 and 1605 the design of the vaulting in the Chamber of Deputies was altered but the spatial arrangement of the room created by Quadro was retained. The complex of parliamentary rooms was also increased with two large entrance halls, on the ground floor in front of the Chamber of Deputies and on the first floor in front of the Senatorial Chamber. Both of these rooms were situated in the new south wing by the Grodzka Gate through which the senators, deputies and public proceeded to the parliamentary rooms. In the entrance halls in front of the Chamber of Deputies and the Senatorial Chamber the Marshal's Hungarians, i.e. a division of the guard clad in Hungarian style uniforms who were under the command of the Royal Grand Marshal, kept guard. Their job was to look after order and security in the parliamentary rooms.

The entrance hall in front of the Chamber of Deputies had a ceiling of arched vaulting with lunettes, supported on two pillars which divided the interior into two parts. This hall was joined with the one in front of the Senatorial Chamber by a monumental double flight of stairs called the Grand Staircase. Its architectural form recalls the Senatorial Staircase in the Wawel which was designed by Trevano between 1599 and 1602. This can thus allow us to assume that the Grand Staircase was the work of the same architect.

The enlargement of the former parliamentary rooms by new entrance halls and a flight of stairs created a complex of large rooms, splendidly suited to their function. These provided the monumental background to the parliamentary pomp and ceremony, especially when the deputies proceeded in solemn procession to the Senatorial Chamber for joint debates with king and senate. The designer of these new Seym rooms was doubtless Trevano.

The decoration of the royal apartments between 1637 and 1645

The area occupied by the royal family was in the north-east wing on the Vistula side and was joined to the Senatorial Chamber by the Grand Entrance Hall. Rooms of a representational-cum-private nature, like the ante-rooms, the Marble Room, the Audience Chamber, the chapel, bedrooms and studies for the royal couple, were situated on the first floor. The royal family also used rooms on the ground and second floors, e.g. the royal bathroom was on the ground floor in the north-east corner, while Ladislaus IV's library was on the second floor above the king's bedroom. In all there were 30 rooms in the royal apartments. Communication between the rooms was effected by four inside staircases. The manner of use of the royal apartments was different at the time of Sigismund III, who had a large family, from that under the other Vasas, Ladislaus IV and John Casimir. Only the function of the grand rooms on the *piano nobile* remained unchanged.

The castle interior acquired rich decorations under Sigismund III and later between 1637 and 1642 at the instigation of Ladislaus IV. The architect who supervised this work was Giovanni Battista Gisleni and the large decorative paintings were executed by the court painter Tommaso Dolabella. The interior was kept in the early Baroque style and modelled on Italian and French residences of the period of Louis XIII. For the first time in Poland architectural divisions of the walls and the principles of symmetry were applied in the castle interior, which were then imitated in all the royal and magnate residences. Expensive decorative techniques, like gilding, were readily used, as were costly materials like marble, the large deposits of which in Chęciny and Dębnik were first exploited on a large scale. The black marble of Dębnik was particularly popular and readily used in Poland at that time.

Floors were made from marble, usually using multi-sided and multi-coloured pieces to form patterns, as were ornate portals and monumental fireplaces. Marble floors and portals were to be found in all the royal apartments on the *piano nobile*. An ornate fireplace with a cast-iron plaque bearing the coats-of-arms of the Commonwealth and the Vasas decorated the Audience Chamber. In the less opulent rooms, like the entrance halls and the chancelleries, beamed ceilings were built, covered with painted decorations of floral and geometric designs or heraldic motifs, and in the official rooms ornate ceilings divided in sections were effected by paintings on canvas. This kind of ceiling with gilded frames and pictures was also found in the first two ante-rooms which led to the Marble Room and the Audience Chamber. In the first one the plafond showed the conquest of Smolensk by Sigismund III in 1609 and in the second one it depicted a scene of the presentation of Tsar Vasili Shuiski as a prisoner by the hetman Stanisław Żółkiewski at the Warsaw Seym in 1611.

An interior with unusual decoration was the Marble Room. A facing of reddish-brown marble from Chęciny and black marble from Dębnik corved its walls. The gilded frames on the ceiling contained a series of historical paintings showing the military victories and diplomatic successes of Ladislaus IV, i.e. the Battle of Chocim in 1621, the peace treaty with Turkey of 1634, a scene from the war with Muscovy of 1610, the Smolensk campaign of 1632, and also the homage of Prussia to Ladislaus IV in 1641 paid by the young Frederick William, later known as Great Elector. Around the room there were 22 portraits of the ancestors and relations which were defined as "the Jagiellonian family" in early inventories. These included pictures of Ladislaus Jagiełło, St. Casimir the Jagiellonian, Sigismund (I) the Old, Catherine the Jagiellonian and her husband John III Vasa, King of Sweden, their son Sigismund III, and his two wives, Anna and Constance, the daughters of the Archduke Charles of Habsburg, and also Ladislaus IV, his wife Cecilia Renata, and her father, the Emperor Ferdinand II. The series ended with a childhood portrait of the son of Ladislaus IV, Prince Sigismund Casimir. The decorations were completed by five cartouches, done in gilded stucco, with the coats-of-arms of Poland, Lithuania, Sweden, the house of Vasa, and of the Grand Duchy of Muscovy of which Ladislaus IV was Tsar-Elect. The theme of the paintings, the heraldic cartouches, and the selection of portraits of the "Jagiellonian family" altogether created a clear dynastic image with which the king wanted to familiarize the gentry community. The series of portraits was supposed to remind them that the Vasas were descended from the native Jagiellonian dynasty and the pictures and coats-of-arms showed what glory the new elected dynasty had bestowed on the

Commonwealth. The hanging of a picture of the king's son, Prince Sigismund Casimir, was significant, too, for it indicated that he was the only heir to the glorious tradition and should one day in the future occupy the now elective throne of the Jagiellonians.

The designer of this unusual room was the afore-mentioned Giovanni Battista Gisleni and the author of the portraits of the "Jagiellonian family" was the Dutch painter Peter Dankers de Rijn who was in royal service. Only the name of the painter of historical pictures remains unknown. However the choice of contents of this room was that of Ladislaus IV himself. Unfortunately the dynastic plan presented here lost its significance in 1646 after the premature death of the king's son in whom the king saw the continuator of the dynasty.

Next to the Marble Room was the Audience Chamber where the royal throne with its canopy was situated. The ceiling was decorated with paintings of Dolabella which illustrated the coronation of Sigismund III in Cracow Cathedral in 1587. This picture was to remind foreign delegations and native border lords of the sacral origin of the authority of the Polish monarchy.

Over the above-mentioned marble fireplace, which was situated opposite the throne, a large equestrian portrait of Sigismund III, also by Dolabella, was probably hung. This type of heroic royal portrait in the shape of a victorious leader was connected with the theme on the ceiling which illustrated his coronation. Around 1639 Dankers de Rijn painted portraits of Ladislaus IV and Queen Cecilia Renata on horseback and after 1649 another equestrian portrait of John Casimir which probably completed the decoration for the Audience Chamber.

In the royal apartments a definite conceptual plan was used. Dolabella's ceilings in the first and second ante-rooms used the theme of the war triumphs of Sigismund III, the Marble Room was devoted to the links between the Polish Vasas and the Jagiellonian dynasty, and the Audience Chamber to the apotheosis of the new dynasty. The completion of the plan was the great painting of Do-labella in the Guards' Hall, opposite the royal dressing room and bedroom and showing the Polish victory against

41

the Turks at the Battle of Chocim in 1621. The subject of this picture warrants our attention as it results from contemporary religious exaltation. Dolabella portrayed the vision which appeared to Father Michael Oborski and was known and discussed widely at that time. In the course of celebrating mass he saw the Virgin Mary and St. Stanislaus Kostka protecting the Polish camp which was surrounded by the Turks. The Polish victory in the Battle of Chocim, in which Prince Ladislaus was the nominal commander-in-chief, became famous all over Europe. To celebrate this success by the Polish army Pope Urban VIII appointed a special holiday on 8 October and Prince Ladislaus was since regarded as a defender of the faith. Dolabella's picture therefore expressed and in a certain way also consolidated the conviction at that time that Poland was the bulwark of Christendom which the saints had undertaken to defend. This subject was connected with the idea of the apotheosis of the Vasa dynasty. The tapestries also served the same purpose, in particular a series of eight hangings illustrating scenes from the Polish-Muscovite war, and another series of battle scenes, of which one tapestry showed the siege of Smolensk. Part of the plan to show the links between the Vasa and Jagiellonian dynasties was also the painting by Krzysztof Boguszewski which illustrated the Battle of Grunwald.

Many tapestries were also hung in the castle rooms. Sigismund III had several series of these hangings in his collection including "A History of the Trojan War", "The Story of Absalom", and "The Story of Saul", which had been commissioned in Brussels by his uncle, Eric XIV, King of Sweden. The court also had at its disposal over 300 tapestries which came from the collection of Sigismund Augustus. One of the series belonging to this collection — "The History of Paradise" — hung in Ladislaus IV's bedroom when he was still only the king's son. Other hangings were also used to decorate the walls. The Dutch diplomat Abraham Boot noticed in 1627 that Queen Constance's room was covered in black velvet. Black was the favourite colour of the early Baroque period in Poland. People dressed in black in accordance with the Spanish fashion and made picture frames, furniture, cupboards, chests, bureaux, and altars for their homes from ebony inlaid with silver. The French diplomat Jean le Laboureur saw the royal apartments in 1646 when he came to Poland in the train of Queen Marie-Louise Gonzaga, Princess of Nevers, who married King Ladislaus IV. M. le Laboureur published his impressions of the visit to Poland in Paris in 1647 under the title of *Relation du voyage de la Reyne de Pologne et du retour de Madame la Mareschalle de Guébriant, ambassadrice extraordinaire et surintendante de sa conduitte...* He wrote that the royal apartments were very beautiful and built completely according to French taste, which for him was certainly the highest compliment possible.

The theatre

In 1637 a new theatrical hall was built in the Castle which early sources call *gran sala di teatro* or *teatro detto di sopra*. The king was a great admirer of Italian operatic theatre and had seen its beginnings between 1624 and 1626 at the courts of Italian princes during his journey as a youth to the countries of Western Europe.

The theatre hall was in the south wing on the second floor. It consisted of a large and long interior containing two floors which were sometimes called galleries and a Frenchman writing under the pseudonym of L'Abbe F.D.S. called it *"une salle en galerie des plus grandes de l'Europe pour jouer les comédies"*.

The length of the room including the stage was about 48 m and its width 12 m. On each of the longer walls there were 16 windows in two rows. The stage had a depth of 24 m. On the sides of the stage were two balconies for the orchestra, with a separate place for the conductor on one of them. Behind the stage there were the dressing rooms.

The architectural framework of the stage opening was effected by a large pillared arch in accordance with the principles of the Italian theatre theoretician Nicola Sabbattini. The stage had a mezzanine and a fly for lowering or raising sets. All equipment and machinery necessary for the Baroque theatre was available and adapted for presenting Italian operas. The stage was connected with the auditorium by a staircase by which the performers could descend to the middle of the hall during the court ballets. From contemporary reports we know that during the performances the king, the royal family, papal nuncio and the Imperial ambassador sat in chairs, placed on a carpet in the centre of the hall. The rest of the audience sat on benches or stood.

The Ladislaus theatre is reminiscent in its architectural form of the court theatres of the Gonzagas in Mantua (1588—89, designed by Vincenzo Scamozzi) and the Farnese family in Parma (1618—28, designed by Giovanni Battista Aleotti) which have been preserved till today. They also had, like the Warsaw theatre, two balconies for the orchestra and a place for honoured guests in the centre of the auditorium. In the castle theatre there were also benches similar to those in the theatres in Florence and in the Paris theatre of Cardinal Mazarin.

The main stage designer of the Ladislaus theatre was Agostino Locci, who bore the title of "His Royal Majesty's Engineer". The technical arrangement of the stage was also built according to his plans and he was certainly assisted by another Italian engineer who was in the service of the king, Bartolomeo Bolzoni. The architectural structure of the auditorium was the work of Giovanni Battista Gisleni who was also the set designer. Sets were also designed by Giacinto Campana and Christian Melich and executed by Jan Hanle, the royal carpenter and wood-carver.

During the whole period of the Vasa dynasty Italian operas were performed in the theatre with stage sets and artificially created effects which frequently aroused the admiration of the audience. As evidence let us quote the opinion of Queen Marie-Louise Gonzaga as expressed in a letter to Cardinal Mazarin: "My mind is so full of a comedy which I just saw that I can't write to you about anything else. I have never seen anything so beautiful before and it was only with difficulty that I would decide to watch the usual French and Italian presentations. This pleasure lasted five hours which seemed to pass in an instant. The music was excellent and the stage effects so astounding that I was really captivated." The Queen wrote these flattering comments in February 1646, i.e. shortly after her arrival in Poland. They refer to an opera entitled *Le Nozze d'Amore e di Psiche* with libretto by Virgilio Puccitelli.

The brave idea of transporting Italian opera to Poland as early as the 1630's and 40's, when in Italy it was going through the period of its early development and only occasionally appeared north of the Alps, bears witness to the high standard of culture at the Polish court. We should not be surprised by the fact that the operatic activities of Ladislaus IV both with regard to the concepts and technical expertise as well as the vocal and musical aspects were entirely the work of Italian engineers, architects, musicians and singers.

Plays were also presented in the Castle theatre as well as operas. In 1639 a travelling group of English actors presented the works of Shakespeare here, certainly for the first time in Poland. An important event in Polish theatrical life was the Polish première of *Le Cid* by Pierre Corneille in the translation of Jan Andrzej Morsztyn which was presented in 1662 with the participation of the ladies of the court of Queen Marie-Louise.

It is also worth bearing in mind the situation of theatre as directly adjacent to the parliamentary rooms. From the time of Ladislaus IV there was the custom at the Polish court that on the occasion of parliamentary sessions the court organized various shows and theatrical performances which were watched by the senators, deputies, and gentry who came for the session. For the greater convenience of the parliamentary audience the auditorium was connected with the Senatorial Vestibule from where a separate flight of stairs led to the upper storey where the theatre was. The performances here were often of a political or even propaganda nature and were one of the ways of shaping national opinion but at the same time popularizing Italian music among fairly broad strata of society.

The extension of the Castle under Ladislaus IV

During the reign of Ladislaus IV a small amount of construction work was undertaken in the Castle. It lasted from 1637 to the mid-1640's, but it had considerable implications for the artistic arrangement of the entire castle layout. A gallery with five arcades was built on to the elevation of the north-east wing on the Vistula side, supporting a terrace which led out from the royal apartments. It can be assumed that this gallery was connected with the planned but never actually effected idea of creating a representational elevation of the Castle facing the garden and the Vistula. The gallery was constructed between the already existing Garden Tower and an irregular outbuilding on the north-east corner. Probably it was intended to build a second tower in place of this outbuilding, identical to the Garden Tower. These two towers would establish the harmony of the arcaded gallery and the terrace situated on it. All palaces built on the Vistula escarpment in the 1640's similarly had constructed garden elevations.

In 1643—4 the magnificent Świętojańska Gate was erected leading to the Front Courtyard which was described above. Both the gallery and the gate were designed by Ladislaus IV's court architect Constantino Tencalla. On one of the bastions which fortified the Vistula bank below the Castle a small palace was built for the king's brother, Prince Charles Ferdinand, Bishop of Płock and Wrocław, at the beginning of the 1640's. This palace was established on a square plan with corner turrets and a tent roof, probably designed by another royal architect, Giovanni Battista Gisleni.

However, the most splendid artistic enterprise of Ladislaus IV was the building of a column in 1644, as a monument in memory of his father and the first Vasa on the throne of Poland. The Sigismund III Column is now situated on the large Castle Square but was originally behind the Cracow Gate and the buildings on the Front Courtyard. The designer of the Column was Constantino Tencalla and the town planner responsible for the layout of the square in front of the Cracow Gate was Agostino Locci. The statue of Sigismund III was made by Clemente Molli and cast in bronze by the Warsaw bell-founder, Daniel Tym.

The Sigismund Column is an extraordinary monument and the only one of its type erected in Europe at that time. It is a well-known fact that in Ancient Rome only statues of emperors were placed on columns which indicated that they were equal to the gods. Two such columns have been preserved in Rome until today — those of Trajan and Marcus Aurelius. In modern times monuments were built in column form in Italy, but only statues of the Virgin Mary or saints were placed on them. In early art the column had various interpretations but was also understood as a monument of supreme glory which was why only divine figures were placed on it. The placing of a royal statue on a column, which was a brave act for those times, is explained by the inscription at the foot of the monument: "King Sigismund III, distinguished in piety and warfare, is justly deserving of two-fold glory", i. e. earthly and heavenly glory. The first is symbolized by the sword in the king's hand, with which he defeated the enemy, and the second by a cross with which he defended Christendom. In the mind of the founder these two virtues justified this elevation of the person of Sigismund III whose military victories and defence of the Faith have become his most important claims to fame. The conviction that military deeds are actions which qualify people for triumphs and apotheosis had been widespread in Poland since the time of the Renaissance. We may add that this conviction was based on Aristotle's *Ethics* who acknowledged heroic bravery — *virtus heroica* — as the only quality which gave a man immortality.

Therefore the Warsaw monument to Sigismund III is so remarkable not only because of its splendid artistic form but also because of its novel conceptual plan recalling ancient culture which was the inspiration for Baroque art in Europe, Poland included.

The devastation of the Castle during the Swedish invasion

The Polish-Swedish war of 1655—6, followed by the occupation of Warsaw by the Swedes and their allies, the Brandenburg Germans, resulted in the devastation of the Castle and the plundering of its art collections. According to Swedish sources King Charles X Gustavus of Sweden removed 300 pictures from the Castle at that time, 33 tapestries of the series "The Story of David", and plafonds from five rooms. The Brandenburgers also looted a lot. According to the contemporary diarist Wawrzyniec Rudawski "the Elector personally took to Prussia the foremost paintings and silver from the royal table as booty". The historical paintings in the Marble Room, Dolabella's picture illustrating the coronation of Sigismund III, and numerous paintings and royal portraits were either removed or destroyed. The rich gallery of paintings collected by Sigismund III and later by Ladislaus IV suffered total dispersal. The Swedes and Brandenburgers even took away the marble fireplaces, door-frames, and marble flooring. Pierre des Noyers, the private secretary to Queen Marie-Louise, made the following comment on the activities of the enemy in one of the letters he wrote at that time: "They scraped the gold off the gilded skirting-boards and then melted down the scrapings to get, at the most, three or four ducats, while doing damage amounting to over 30,000; in all their activities they displayed supreme greed."

At that time several buildings of the so-called Old Castle were burned down — those which ran along the Vistula escarpment and the palace of Prince Charles Ferdinand, which was never rebuilt and ruins of which were not finally removed until the beginning of the 18th century. By the end of the war the Castle had been completely devastated and as M. des Noyers wrote: "The Swedes damaged the Castle so much that it is no longer fit for habitation. They even brought in horses to the rooms on the third floor. Everywhere is full of the ordure and corpses of Swedish soldiers."

The Castle was quickly put in order, however, and made ready for parliaments and the work of the various royal departments. In the royal apartments only a few parts of the former artistic decorations remained, including the "Jagiellonian family" portraits in the Marble Room, the Dolabella ceilings showing the Conquest of Smolensk and Homage by Tsar Vasili Shuiski in the ante-rooms, and the Victory of Chocim in the Guards' Hall. Redecoration of the royal apartments was carried out after 1657 but did not attain the previous level of artistic expression and content. The apartment walls were covered with tapestries which were frequently admired by foreigners. Sigismund Augustus' collection of tapestries did not hang in the Castle at this time as it had been saved from the Swedes and pawned by John Casimir with bankers in Gdańsk. We know that one of the Castle rooms was decorated with a large number of mirrors for a court celebration in 1659. After the Swedish wars the royal apartments were only used by the court on the occasion of large receptions. John Casimir and Marie-Louise lived mainly in the *Villa Regia,* later known as the Casimir Palace (*Pałac Kazimie- rzowski*). The remains of the castle collections which did not form a permanent part of the rooms were taken with him by John Casimir when he went to France after his abdication in 1669.

The next elected king, Michael Korybut Wiśniowiecki, took over the royal apartments stripped completely bare. At the end of 1669 work was carried out on the temporary decoration of the royal rooms and their adaptation as the new royal residence. However during the short reign of King Michael Korybut no major operations were undertaken. Work on decorating the Castle interior was next carried out under his successor, King John III Sobieski.

THE CASTLE UNDER JOHN III

The royal bath-house

During the reign of John III Sobieski (1674—96) work was carried out on the interiors of the royal apartments and the parliamentary rooms. The former Grand En- trance Hall and Guards' Hall in the royal rooms were divided into smaller rooms. Further partitions were carried out in the private rooms on the second floor. This work was supervised by Agostino Locci the Younger, the son of the engineer and architect mentioned above who worked for Ladislaus IV. Agostino Locci the Younger was there- fore the second generation of Italian artists settled in Warsaw and working at the Polish court. The Castle exterior remained in its original early Baroque form. The only building which to a certain extent relieved the fundamentalist architecture of the Castle was the turning of the former Garden Tower which was sited in the north-east wing on the Vistula side into the Royal Bath-house pavilion. This pavilion was designed in 1681 by Locci. The Royal Bath-house erected by him was a smallish, two-storey building, decorated on the ground floor with pillars, arcades, and niches in which to erect statues, surmounted by a balustrade. The second floor was a superstructure in the form of a gloriette with three large windows finished off with the curved section, which was covered by a cupola topped with a decorative jardi-niere. The decorative and pleasing effects of the chiaros-curo architectural form of the Bath-house pavilion was typical of the architecture of the mature Baroque period and in certain parts was reminiscent of Wilanów Palace which was also built by Locci.

On the ground floor of the pavilion was a bathroom with a bath and a dressing room from where winding stairs led to the interior of the gloriette where there was a room, with rounded corners and a fountain in the middle, which was perhaps designed in the style of a grot-to. Because of the large windows through which there was an extensive view of the Castle garden and the Vistula, this room was called the Glass Room.

The Royal Bath-house was a pavilion in the style of a *maison de plaisance* or *ermitorium* which became fashionable all over Europe in the second half of the 18th century under the influence of the garden buildings at Versailles. A series of pavilions containing a bathroom, dressing rooms, and bedrooms, intended for bathing, meditation, and indoor entertainments, was designed by the illustrious architect working in Poland at that time, Tylman van Gameren. These, however, were park pavil-ions, built separately, and usually erected at some distance from the main residence. On the other hand the Castle Bath-house in the former Garden Tower was connected to the state rooms and private apartments of the king but owing to its separation from the main sequence of rooms it partly played the role of a *maison de plaisance*. We know from old accounts that John III Sobieski very much liked to work and spend his free time in this building.

The most important construction work which was effected with excellent artistic quality was the rebuilding of the parliamentary rooms between 1678 and 1681. Part of this rebuilding involved the transfer of the Chamber of Deputies from the ground floor of the former Large House to the first floor of the west wing. The Large House ceased to be a building exclusively intended for parliamentary work and both parliamentary rooms were now situated in the *piano nobile* wings, i.e. the west, south, and south-east. The entrance to the new Chamber of Deputies was by the monumental staircase situated in the west wing in the Sigismund Tower. This staircase, which was bipolar, was constructed at the beginning of the 17th century but was only at this period connected with the parliamentary rooms and as a result took on the name of the Deputies' Staircase. It was used by both the delegates and the public. Before the Chamber of Deputies came a large entrance hall which covered the entire width of the west wing. It was there that the Marshal's Hungarians kept guard.

New architectural alterations were carried out in the Chamber of Deputies at this time. It was built as an almost square-shaped rectangle. On the north wall was a platform surrounded by a balustrade where the parliamentary secretaries and "those deputed to inscribe laws and statutes" sat. Below this platform was the seat of the Speaker who chaired the debates. The deputies' benches were arranged in a semi-circle around the other three walls. The centre of the room was left bare. The public could listen to the debates while standing behind the deputies' benches.

The walls of the Chamber were covered by mono-chrome decoration fashioned in stucco which was made up of panoplies composed of various weapons. Above the doors in the longer walls were two maps, those of the Kingdom of Poland and the Grand Duchy of Lithuania. The wall above the secretaries' platform had stucco decoration in the form of an outstretched drapery with a pelmet at the top. This drapery was held by an eagle's talons and on the sides it was garlanded with two bunches of oak and palm leaves. This decoration emphasized the highest point of the Chamber from where the Speaker presided over the debates and where the statutes were written down.

The Chamber of Deputies was connected with the Senatorial Chamber by a set of rooms, i.e. by a gallery situated in the south wing which contained two large halls intended as a chancellery and a conference room. The delegates proceeded through this gallery to the joint debates in the Senatorial Chamber. In the new layout of the parliamentary rooms the role of the Grand Staircase was changed as it was now only used by the senators. The remaining rooms in the south wing were unchanged. As before, the Senatorial Chamber was preceded by the Large Hall and the Senatorial Vestibule and a chapel in the Grodzka Tower.

As in the Chamber of Deputies, new stucco work decoration was put up in the Senatorial Chamber too. The most significant part of it from the point of view of content was concentrated on the wall behind the throne. A canopy over the throne was made of stucco, shaped in the form of a pinned, patterned drapery with a Polish eagle with outstretched wings on it whose breast bore the Janina coat-of-arms of the Sobieski family. Over the doors on the sides of the throne were shields with the emblems of Poland and Lithuania, covered in rich decorations consisting of piles of ornaments and fruit, and mythological figures blowing on trumpets. The Janina coat-of-arms motif also appeared on the overdoors on the breast of the Polish eagle and as a shield, held by the rider in the Lithuanian emblem. Both heraldic shields were surmounted by the Polish royal and the Lithuanian grand ducal crowns. Below the ceiling the room was encircled with garlands of leaves, fruit, and flowers.

The stucco decorations in the Deputies' and Senatorial Chambers described above were destroyed at the beginning of the 18th century during the Northern War (1700-21). We only know what these rooms looked like from iconographic drawings which allow us to judge the artistic standard of the stucco work which covered them. We can only guess that they were decorated by the same Italian artists and stucco craftsmen who at the same time decorated the royal palace at Wilanów, the Bieliński residence at Otwock, the Krasiński residence in Warsaw, the church at Czerniaków, and other buildings in Warsaw. Without doubt the artistic level of the stucco work in the parliamentary rooms was equal to the decoration preserved in the above-mentioned residences and churches. In addition, the series of motifs which appeared in the Castle, like the panoplies, festoons and draperies, are analogous to those in Wilanów Palace, which suggests that both works were the product of one artist or one workshop.

The iconographic drawings of the parliamentary rooms also enable us to see the conceptual plan imposed on the rooms in the reign of John III.

The decoration of the parliamentary rooms and the conceptual plan behind the contents in them were derived from the artistic, historical and philosophical trends of the Baroque period, an expression of which was the belief that the Polish gentry were descended from the ancient Romans. This view was originally held by a small intellectual elite of magnates but was quickly accepted and adopted as their own by the broad strata of the gentry. There arose a general belief in the rebirth of Roman virtues in the Polish gentry, conspicuous evidence of which was to be the Commonwealth, the only legacy of the governmental system of the Roman Republic. The native Polish tradition, often even the family tradition, but above all the native governmental tradition were seen as being derived from antiquity. This trend was expressed in the sphere of art by a decided tendency to "antiquate" form and content.

An expression of these very tendencies was the conceptual plan of the parliamentary rooms which clearly reflected, within the understanding of every deputy and even every nobleman, the system of government of the Commonwealth.

The panoplies adorning the Chamber of Deputies, composed of items of knights' weaponry and military insignia, and the old style armour linked with the contemporary weapons which had been taken by the Poles from the Muslim East, were supposed to underline the function of the hall in which representatives of gentry society, designating themselves as a knights' estate, took part in debates. War trophies were also shown on the panoply. In ancient times captured arms were hung on stakes driven into the ground — the *tropaeum* — from which the frequently used divisional arrangement of panoply decoration was derived. The *tropaea* in the Chamber of Deputies were intended to symbolise past victories and the endeavours of the gentry in maintaining the defence of the country, thus creating to a certain extent the popular idea that "our bodies stand firm as walls and castles". Within such a definite idea the draperies hung in the two chambers had not only a decorative significance. They represented the ancient Roman mantle, the *paludamentum*, which belonged to the leading generals and emperors. This was a short cloak, thrown over the shoulders and fastened on the right one. The emperor was entitled to a purple cloak, decorated with embroidery, and the generals a white one. When the troops were encamped, the *paludamentum,* hung on stakes, created a sort of back of the canopy against the background of which the commander sat for military conferences and ceremonies. The *paludamentum* hanging in the Chamber of Deputies over the Speaker's seat and the parliamentary secretaries was understood in the same way. In this room the Speaker was the first man in council and the first man of the knights' estate, and therefore like a commander. The eagle holding the *paludamentum* is defined in handbooks of symbolic art as the personification of authority and power, the attributes by which the gentry and their representatives debating in the Chamber of Deputies were supposed to be distinguished. Bunches of palm leaves symbolizing *honos* and *virtus*, i.e. honour and bravery, qualities which the gentry had acquired in their defence of the Commonwealth, were hung over the Speaker's chair and these ensured the state's everlasting glory, which was marked by branches of laurel within the panoply. The interior was decorated like an ancient military camp ready for what was known as a minor triumph as indicated by the *tropaea* with the captured weaponry and the outstretched *paludamentum*. Another link with ancient times was the amphitheatrical arrangement of the deputies' benches, which was used for the first time in the Polish Seym. A factor which showed that the above contents referred to a particular period in the history of Poland were the two maps of the same size of the Kingdom of Poland and the Grand Duchy of Lithuania. They also showed that the representatives of two federated nations were debating here.

A development of the idea depicted in the Chamber of Deputies was the decoration in the Senatorial Chamber, the plan of which, while derived from antiquity, emphasized more the current situation in the state, its structure and above all its sovereignty with regard to the other courts of Europe. It also clearly revealed the dynastic aspirations of Sobieski.

An item preserved from antiquity was the patterned *paludamentum* to which the commander-in-chief and ruler — the emperor — was entitled. The *paludamentum* was hung as a canopy over the royal throne in the Senatorial Chamber and was an artistic realization of the motto: *Rex imperator in regno suo.* Stretched out on the back of the canopy was an heraldic eagle with the Janina coat-of-arms of the Sobieski family on its breast which personified the one monarch of the Commonwealth, the King of Poland. On the sides of the throne there were to be seen cartouches on the overdoors with the coats-of-arms of Poland and Lithuania which indicated two countries joined together in one Commonwealth of the Two Nations.

Apart from these obvious, unequivocal contents there was also another element among the decorations in the Senatorial Chamber which apotheosized the person of the king and the possible future dynasty. The festoons on the walls and the bunches of fruit and flowers on the overdoors symbolized the bountiful harvests under the fortunate rule of John III. Shields with the Janina coat-of-arms of the Sobieskis on the breast of the Polish eagle and held by the rider of the Lithuanian emblem, indicated that this prosperity covered both Poland and Lithuania. According to the handbooks of symbolic art the shield is also the symbol of protection. In this case the Janina shields were to indicate the protection by the king or rather the future Sobieski dynasty of the Commonwealth and these important facts were announced by mythological figures, blowing on trumpets.

The rooms inhabited by the royal family at this time were decorated with various tapestries and hangings, both oriental and West-European, which John III had in his large collection. This collection also consisted of 14 Jagiellonian tapestries which were bought back from the pawn shops in Gdańsk and which were seen at the Castle in 1683 by the French poet Jean François Regnard. We know that the bedroom of Queen Marie-Casimire was covered with crimson velvet with gores of a silver flowery material, and the king's bedroom had a series of eight gobelin hangings, woven with gold thread with scenes of various battles, which had been given to him by Elector Maximilian II Emmanuel of Bavaria. The decoration of the Audience Chamber was another example of the influence of ancient times which was so popular in Polish art at that time. The walls of the Chamber were covered with hangings made of green velvet with representations of Roman emperors, doubtless done by an embroidery technique. We may assume that the French traveller the Abbé F.D.S. gave an honest opinion when he said that "the tapestries in the Castle are the most beautiful in the world".

PLANS AND ALTERATIONS TO THE CASTLE IN THE FIRST HALF OF THE 18TH CENTURY

Work carried out between 1710 and 1726

In 1697 Frederick Augustus, the Elector of Saxony, was elected to the Polish throne and took the name of Augustus II, King of Poland. He got the Commonwealth entangled in the lengthy Northern War. At this time Warsaw was often occupied by Swedish, Saxon, and Russian armies, or the Polish forces of the followers of Augustus II or of Stanislaus Leszczyński who was elected king in 1704. At this time the Castle suffered neglect and devastation and was particularly badly damaged during the assault of September 1704 by Polish-Saxon forces who attacked the Swedes who held it at that time. The corner turrets on the façade, the Grodzka Tower, the annexe topped with a cupola, which housed the chapel presbytery, and the south wing with the theatre hall were all destroyed. The interior suffered utter devastation, including both parliamentary rooms with their stucco decorations. Also the last two Dolabella ceilings which adorned the royal ante-rooms disappeared.

In 1705 the Castle was renovated for the coronation of Stanislaus Leszczyński who resided there for a short period together with his family, including his daughter Marie who later became Queen of France as the wife of Louis XV. The events of the next few years, however, resulted in the Castle being reduced to its previous state of devastation.

A period of relative domestic tranquillity returned to Poland in 1710 when Augustus II regained the throne after the defeat of Charles XII of Sweden at the Battle of Poltava. Various repairs were carried out in the Castle in 1713, and in 1716 a new theatre hall was built in the so-called Old Castle. At the same time, probably around 1715, a splendid plan was drawn up on the instigation of Augustus II for a complete rebuilding of the Castle with the late Baroque style retained. This plan envisaged the addition of an extended middle part with two side projections to the former pentagon of the monumental wing on the Vistula side. The Sigismund Tower and all the elevations around the Grand Courtyard were to be rebuilt. On the slope of the escarpment a large garden was to be laid out, in the French style, enclosed on two sides by low side wings and turreted pavilions. Unfortunately we do not know the name of the architect who designed this plan. It was attributed to the Dresden architects Matthaeus Daniel Pöppelmann or Johann Friedrich Karcher but both suggestions are not accepted today. Anyway the plan was never put into practice.

The work carried out on the Castle over the next few years had a considerably more modest range. Between 1721 and 1726 the royal apartments were rebuilt, making use of the partitioning walls constructed here at the time of John III, thanks to which the royal rooms had regained the same format that they had had under the Vasas. The walls of the rooms were covered in red velvet with gold braid, new stoves and fireplaces were built, and also panelling with modest French Regency decoration was provided.

The rebuilding of the Senatorial Chamber

In 1721 the rebuilding of the Senatorial Chamber was also begun and it was raised by one storey. The plan was the work of the French architect, Zacharias Longuelune, who came from Berlin to the Polish court in 1715. The new room acquired a rich architectural decoration. On the side walls of the first floor were double pillars which enclosed six deep window recesses. Between the pillars were pedestals which supported busts of Roman emperors. The recesses above the windows contained the coats-of-arms of the lands of the Commonwealth, which were painted by the Warsaw artist Jan Karnersdorfer. On the second floor above the window bays were seats for arbitrators and between them decorative *panneaux* which acted as emblems of authority for the dignitaries of Poland and Lithuania. On the wall opposite the throne was a large map of the Commonwealth made from multi-coloured marble. Over the doors were the coats-of-arms of Poland and Lithuania in richly-worked cartouches, and on one of the longer walls a monumental statue of Augustus II was designed to go in a shell-shaped niche. A setting for the throne designed by Longuelune with extraordinary splendour in the shape of an altar or a shrine was never built. The senators and deputies opposed the execution of this plan, reading into this excessive elevation of the royal person the absolutist and dynastic aspirations of the Wettin (Saxon) dynasty. The statue of the king was not executed either.

The decoration of the Senatorial Chamber was one of the most splendid artistic creations to appear in Warsaw in the first quarter of the 18th century. Its design and in fact the whole work of Longuelune was derived from the grand French style of the time of Louis XIV, but it also possessed more delicate and decorative forms which were due to the influence of the Regency style.

According to the original idea imposed by the king and worked on by Longuelune, the Senatorial Chamber had a definite plan of contents. However, not all the details of this plan are legible today. Doubtless the main idea was the apotheosis of the monarch as expressed by the statue of Augustus II and the busts the eight emperors placed between the window recesses which created a sort of idealized genealogy of the king. The decoration of the Senatorial Chamber included also motifs referring to the myth of Hercules as the personification of heroic bravery — *virtus heroica* — which was very popular in the late Baroque period. Augustus II liked to see himself in the form of Hercules, as heroic bravery according to the Baroque view of antiquity was the characteristic which could raise man to the rank of *heros*, i.e. a divine-like figure. Hence a setting for the throne reminiscent of an altar was to be placed in the Senatorial Chamber. Therefore it can be assumed that in general outline the plan of contents for the Chamber was in the original design the apotheosis of the king as hero who in bliss and prosperity ruled over the Commonwealth which was symbolized by heraldic emblems and the arms of dignitaries. What was finally constructed from this design was a form of compromise between the absolutist aspirations of a foreign king and his tendency to deify his own person on the one hand, and the republican Commonwealth and its own gentry democracy on the other.

In the 1720's and 30's Longuelune put into effect several other designs inside the Castle including a lovely plan for the Royal Bedroom.

Plans and construction of the main building on the Vistula side

An extensive rebuilding of the Castle was undertaken in the 1740's during the reign of Augustus III (1734—63). It is worth drawing attention here to the reasons which brought about the rebuilding and modernization of the Castle. It had been a long respected custom for the king to live at the Castle during the parliamentary sessions. The gentry demanded that the king reside there and "conduct his court" as was said in those days. However, both kings of the Saxon house of Wettin, Augustus II and Augustus III, usually lived in their own private palace in Warsaw, the so-called Saxon Palace (*Pałac Saski*), or in other suburban residences. During the parliamentary sessions they only came to the Castle to attend the sessions and the royal apartments remained empty and bare. The court explained that the Castle was too confined, the majority of rooms were occupied by various government offices, and the royal family did not have suitable accommodation there. Therefore the Seym and government departments decided to increase the size of the Castle and create suitable rooms for the royal family.

With this end in view the Italian architect Gaetano Chiaveri was engaged and had come to Warsaw from St. Petersburg towards the end of the 1720's. In 1737 or perhaps a little earlier he drafted a design for a new main building on the Vistula side to which he gave the form of a separate palace building, superbly joined on to the wings of the former pentagonal structure. The elevation on the east side of the new main block had three projections jutting out to the front, joined to each other by cloisters. The central projection was surmounted by a high gable with the arms of the Commonwealth and the house of Wettin on it. Chiaveri designed several slightly different version of the plan. Initially, the best plan was certainly chosen, but as a result of further work the plan was changed a little bit and the central projection was altered by rounding off its corners and replacing the high gable with a low parapet which bore a tablet with an inscription and an heraldic cartouche. It was not Chiaveri who made these changes and it can only be assumed that is was Zacharias Longuelune. The construction work began in 1741 without the help of Chiaveri who in 1738 had been commissioned by Auguśtus III to build a Catholic Church for the court in Dresden. The work on the Castle lasted until 1746 and was directed by the Warsaw architect Antoni Solari who held the office of "architect of His Royal Majesty and the Commonwealth", part of whose duties was the supervision of construction work carried out by the state authorities, including the Warsaw Castle. Solari was descended from a family of Italian architects which had been settled in Poland for some generations and had been completely polonized. The buildings constructed by him, which are still in existence today, bear witness to his rare talent. We can assume that during the construction of the Castle he introduced various changes in the plans described above. The sculptural decorations which adorned the exterior elevations of the new central block in the rococo style, which was fashionable at that time, were carried out in two stages in 1741—42 and 1752 by the splendid Warsaw sculptor, Jan Jerzy Plersch.

The building of the main block on the Vistula side was only part of the intended extension and modernization of the castle layout. Two years earlier, in 1738, a new kitchen building was erected in accordance with the plan of Chiaveri in the kitchen courtyard (it was demolished in the middle of the 19th century). The demolition of the Ladislaus Tower and replacing it with a representational façade on the Grand Courtyard side was also planned. It was also intended to make alterations to the early Baroque elevations of the remaining wings of the pentagon. On the site of the Old Castle the construction of a new east wing was planned which together with the existing south-east wing would enclose the monumental main block to form a symmetrical composition. Out of all of these plans only the building of a new south elevation on the north wing facing the Grand Courtyard was put into effect, and a low annexe was constructed between 1748 and 1750 at the foot of the escarpment.

Of the work on the Castle planned and carried out between 1737 and 1746, the highest artistic level was attained by the main block on the Vistula side. Its mass and façade which stood completely apart from the castle building created a sort of separate palace building. From the point of view of scale and function it was the largest and most monumental residence to be built in Poland in the first half of the 18th century. Ultimately the shape of the main block and the façade were reminiscent of French classical Baroque. The main castle block is undoubtedly a unique, original creation for which it is difficult to find a prototype. Chiaveri and Longuelune here adapted French ideas to existing spatial conditions and local needs.

The originality of the building is further intensified by the imaginative and whimsical rococo sculptural decorations which are affixed to the neo-classical architecture in small framed sections. The sculptor Jan Jerzy Plersch had a role equal to the architect in the creation of the building and its stylistic expression.

The sculptural decorations and stucco works which adorned the façade of the new main block were based on a conceptual design which showed in no uncertain manner that this was the first building in the state. In the plan worked out by Chiaveri the high gable over the central projection was topped by the heraldic cartouches of Poland, Lithuania, and the house of Wettin in the framework of richly fashioned war trophies. The gable was surmounted by a statue of Minerva in a helmet with spear and aegis. In the gables over the side projections, were cartouches with the initials of Augustus III and his spouse, Queen Maria Josepha, supported by mythological figures blowing trumpets. In Baroque symbolic art Minerva usually symbolized victory. This decoration illustrated the apotheosis of a triumphant Commonwealth of the Two Nations under the prosperous rule of the royal couple, and the figures announced abroad news of this apotheosis.

In the form of the design that was actually built the sculptural arrangement of the central projection was altered but this did not change its conceptual significance. The parapet bore a tablet with the inscription AUGUST III P.P. INSTAVRARI ET ORNARI CVRAVIT MDCCXLVI (Augustus III, Father of the Nation, commissioned this building and decorations in 1746), and above it was a cartouche with the coat-of-arms of the Commonwealth and the coat-of-arms of the house of Wettin on a heart-shaped shield. The cartouche was surmounted by the royal crown and supported by war trophies composed of "antiquitized" weapons fixed on stakes, helmets, shields, and rifle barrels wreathed with palm branches; nearby was a representation of a lamb. Beneath the cartouche hung the cross of the Order of the White Eagle. On the sides of the parapet with the inscription and the cartouche were two female figures — one in royal garb girdled with the sash of the Order of the White Eagle and near her a cherub supporting the crown and eagle with outspread wings representing Poland; and the other supported on a cartouche under the grand ducal crown with the symbol of Lithuania and, running in front of her, a cherub holding a bunch of fasces, signifying Lithuania. Below the inscribed tablet and above the middle windows of the *piano nobile* was a cartouche under a crown in an uneven rococo shape with the initials AR3 supported by a cherub. War trophies composed of pieces of armour, helmets and palm leaves also wreathed the rounded corners of the central projection and the triangular gables of the side projections.

The war trophies set on stakes arranged in an ancient style symbolized the triumph of the Commonwealth. Its allegorical significance was created by two female figures, Poland and Lithuania, and the heraldic cartouche sur-mounted by the crown looming over the whole com-position. The lamb near the cartouche was an animal sacrificed by ancient peoples to the gods during triumphs. Another inseparable attribute for triumphs were palm branches which richly decorated the cartouches and trophies.

This design, in accordance with the republican prin-ciples of government, illustrated not the triumph of the individual but the apotheosis of the Commonwealth and indirectly the entire gentry estate of the two nations. Thus the person of the sovereign was discreetly indicated only by the coat-of-arms of the Wettin dynasty on a heart-shaped shield and the cartouche with the initials of the king over the central window.

The conceptual design of the façade of the main block could only have arisen locally outside the immediate surroundings of Augustus III to whom the contents displayed here were foreign and unimportant. The design illustrated the view universally held by the gentry of the role of the state and the king. The foundation stone in the parapet of the central projection has the form of a con-ventional invocation usually used in particularly solemn inscriptions and does not have to signify at all that the building was in fact erected and decorated on the orders of the Father of the Nation. The conceptual expression of the new main block was certainly imposed by one of the royal dignitaries for the rebuilding of the official royal residence and the origin of this design should be sought in the indigenous artistic culture which arose at the court of John III. A similar conceptual design was carried out in the second half of the 18th century in both parliamentary rooms.

The royal apartments

The rooms in the new main block were intended exclusively for the use of the king. The main entrance led through the Senatorial Gate in the old north wing, then up a staircase designed by Chiaveri to a gallery with rooms belonging to the royal children and to a large ante-room. This ante-room came in front of the large two storey Audience Chamber with rounded corners which was in the central projection of the newly built block. In the south projection was the bedroom of the royal couple. The king's dressing rooms and ante-room were connected with it. In the north projection a large two storey chapel with a rounded apse was planned. The refined architecture of this room, which had been partly preserved until recently, displayed stylistic links with the work of Longuelune. Near the chapel was a dining-room next door to the Marshal's dining room or so-called "second table".

However in the new main block there was no room for apartments for Queen Maria Josepha. To provide them, the Senatorial Chamber was transferred from the south-east wing to the west one where the Chamber of Deputies had previously been. Thus the west wing — facing the town — became a sort of separate Seym building and the wings on the side of the escarpment were intended exclusively for royal habitation. In place of the previous Senatorial Chamber and the halls in front of it a large suite of rooms for the queen was built going from the Grand Staircase to the junction with the new main block. The queen's rooms were preceded by two ante-rooms. In the Grodzka Tower there were two studies. From a third ante-chamber there was an entrance to the queen's Audience Chamber. Beyond that were four rooms — studies and dressing rooms — attached to the bedroom of the royal couple.

The new rooms for the king and queen were decorated in rococo style. One of the queen's studies was decorated in 1746 with stucco work made by the Warsaw sculptor Józef Sendlinger. In the other rooms there was panelling painted in white or yellow with gilded borders and ornamentation. On the overdoors were pictures representing flowers or figural scenes and over the stone or marble fireplaces hung large mirrors with gilded frames. The walls in some of the rooms were covered in silk, usually in a millefleur pattern, and the third ante-chamber of the queen and the studies in the Grodzka Tower had wall painting decoration which imitated small architectural sections. The Audience Chambers of the king and queen were covered in red velvet decorated with gold braid. In the rooms there were also decorated painted stoves described in early inventories as Saxon or Polish ones.

The new arrangement of the parliamentary rooms and the conversion of the Deputies' Chamber

The transfer of the Senatorial Chamber to the west wing and the separation of the private apartments from the noisy parliamentary rooms was certainly advantageous to the peace of the court and the royal family. At the same time this decision resulted in a network of rooms intended for public use. The arrangement of the parliamentary rooms that was put into effect at the beginning of the reign of Augustus III has been maintained until the present day. The new Senatorial Chamber acquired almost the same shape and dimensions as previously. It also had the same design. Therefore the architectural decoration designed by Longuelune in the form of pillars, panelling, emblems, etc., was transferred in their entirety and refitted in the new site. This work was supervised by the royal architect Daniel Jauch. Thus the new chamber was constructed in the same way as the old one and with only minor changes lasted until the 19th century. The Senatorial Chamber was preceded by an extended square-shaped hall called The Marshal's Guards' Room to which two studies intended as chancelleries were attached. The entrance to the parliamentary rooms was by the former Deputies' Staircase which was not altered. This is the way the deputies and public came in. On the other hand the entrance for the senators was in the north wing and proceeded through the former rooms of the royal children, now called the first, second, and third senatorial ante-rooms. The large hall in front of the Chamber of Deputies by the staircase was divided into three parts: a kind of gallery connecting the chamber with the staircase and two chancellery rooms. In the Chamber of Deputies at this time a colonnade of 14 pillars was erected which went round the room on all four sides.

The next rebuilding of the Chamber of Deputies took place between 1762 and 1764. The reason for this work was the uproar in the Seym in 1762 created by fighting between opposing parties. This led to an intervention by the arbitrators, the flourishing of swords and pistols and as a result to the dissolution of the Seym.

Straight after the disturbance a senatorial council was assembled which decided to erect a public gallery in the Chamber of Deputies to prevent the deputies coming into contact with the arbitrators; a special separate entrance would lead to the gallery and a separate deputies' entrance would lead to the debating chamber. The designer of the new hall was the architect of the Royal Treasury, Jakub Fontana, and the man who carried it out was the Warsaw carpenter, Gottlieb Jentz. The Chamber of Deputies was raised by one storey and in accordance with the decree of the senatorial council a gallery along three walls of the Chamber was built and on the fourth side a staircase was constructed which was reached from a vestibule. Over the staircase was a kind of amphitheatre for the public and beyond it another small balcony supported on four pillars. The gallery running round the hall had a wooden balustrade decorated with cartouches with the coats-of-arms of the lands and provinces in the Commonwealth, made by Jan Jerzy Plersch and, above the cartouches, with palm trees which were sculpted in wood and painted green. The hall contained 18 senatorial benches arranged in a semi-circle, the Speaker's seat, and a table for the parliamentary secretary covered in red cloth. The ceiling was decorated with stucco work and paintings with panoply motifs. In the middle hung a large wooden chandelier for 38 candles adorned with sculpted flowers and laurels. The gallery balustrades were painted grey as an imitation of marble and the wainscoting covering the walls had panels painted grey and green.

In front of the Chamber of Deputies was a large vestibule with a ceiling supported on two columns. The walls were broken up by pillars and panels and all around the benches were painted walnut brown. The vestibule played the role of a guardroom and waiting room for the parliamentary room. Two separate entrances led from it to the Chamber of Deputies and one led up to a staircase by which the public reached the gallery.

There is a large number of written records about the rebuilding of the Chamber of Deputies but Fontana's plans have not been preserved. The only iconographic record is the drawing by Jean Pierre Norblin of 1786 which shows the Chamber of Deputies with galleries, an amphitheatre supported by pillars, and balcony and palm trees.

The palm trees which were used for the decoration of the Chamber are worthy of special comment. Palm motifs were popular and widespread in rococo decorations, both in Poland and in other European countries. They were normally linked with the elaborate floral ornamentations characteristic of rococo art. In all of these decorations they only served to adorn the interior by heightening the impression of fantasy and exoticism, and if they had any significance, it was limited to that of casual amusement and temporary diversion. However in the palms decorating the Chamber of Deputies it is possible to read another, deeper meaning.

According to the handbooks of symbolic art the palm is a symbol of honour and virtue, more exactly bravery, i.e. the personification of *honos* and *virtus*. In his book *Omnia... Emblemata* published in 1618, Andrea Alciato wrote that just as a bent palm cannot be broken but always lives and grows higher and higher, so the quality of bravery put to the test hardens and results in victory. Bravery and honour were the virtues possessed by the gentry according to contemporary ideas. The palm trees in the Chamber of Deputies should therefore be understood as *palmae virtutis*, i.e. an expression of honour and bravery, the qualities of the gentry estate. The palms were placed on the gallery balustrade as if they grew out of the bas-relief and painted heraldic cartouches of the lands and provinces of the Commonwealth.

This indicated the fact that not only were the delegates of the provinces assembled here but also the qualities which the palm symbolized were rooted in the knights' estate in the regions illustrated by coats-of-arms. Something else connected with this conceptual image were the panoplies painted on the ceiling symbolizing spoils of war, an inseparable attribute of the knights' estate. We do not know what was depicted in the other painting and stucco works but certainly they were linked to the same theme of the conceptual plan of which only a few fragments are extant today. The conceptual expression of the room was a link with the plan of the room under John III.

THE RESIDENCE OF
STANISLAUS AUGUSTUS

A court of artists

Stanislaus Augustus Poniatowski who was elected king in 1764 was the most famous patron of the arts ever to sit on the Polish throne and one of the most illustrious of the monarchs of Europe at that time. Of the numerous, varied cultural and artistic projects initiated by the king the planned rebuilding of the entire Castle complex holds pride of place. The king's intentions lay in three areas: the alteration of the urban layout around the Castle; the construction of new buildings for the Seym; and the creation of royal apartments, both for public and private use. The king only managed to put into effect the last of these intentions. The other projects remained only on paper. However, they contributed to the development of Polish architecture at the end of the 18th and the beginning of the 19th century and today, fortunately preserved, they bear witness to the high level of artistic culture at the Poniatowski court.

Stanislaus Augustus gathered round him a numerous and excellent court of artists. "The architect of His Royal Majesty and the Commonwealth" was Jakub Fontana and, after his death in 1773, Domenico Merlini took over his position. Other famous architects working for the king were Jan Chrystian Kamsetzer, Efraim Szreger, and later Jakub Kubicki and Stanisław Zawadzki. The leader of the entire artists' entourage and adviser on all the artistic plans of Stanislaus Augustus was Marcello Bacciarelli. Other painters closely connected with the court were Jean Pillement, Jan Bogumił Plersch, Józef Ścisło, Franciszek Smuglewicz, Kazimierz Wojniakowski, and the sculptors André Le Brun, Jakub Monaldi, and Józef Pinck. Famous foreign, mainly Parisian, artists also worked for Stanislaus Augustus, e.g. the architect Victor Louis, the decorator Jean Louis Prieur, the gold and bronze experts François-Thomas Germain, Philipe Caffiéri, Etienne Maurice Falconet, and the cabinet-maker Louis Delanois and others.

Plans for the alteration of the interior of the main Castle block

The first plan for rebuilding the Castle was drawn up in 1764 by Jakub Fontana. He intended to demolish all the buildings in the Front Courtyard and create a large Courtyard of Honour with an irregular shape in its place. The main emphasis for the new courtyard was to be a portico with six columns to be added on to the façade. Victor Louis presented a more radical plan in 1765 and even made a special journey from Paris to Warsaw to get acquainted with the topography of the site. In place of the irregular buildings in front of the Castle he planned a monumental construction with an oval square in front of the Castle façade and an avenue situated on a line with the Sigismund Tower. On the Grand Courtyard in place of the Ladislaus Tower he planned a palatial façade. Between 1766 and 1772 Jakub Fontana drew up another four plans for altering the Castle and its surroundings and the king later entrusted similar tasks to Merlini (1773—88) and Szreger (1777). Szreger's design was marked by forcefulness and monumentality in particular, for he intended to build a triumphal arch, an equestrian statue of Stanislaus Augustus, and another column with a statue of John III on it to accompany the already existing column to Sigismund III, in front of the Castle. The view of the square and Krakowskie Przedmieście was to be finished off with an enormous church on the plan of a Greek cross with a dome.

None of these plans were ever put into effect, but if they had been, despite the inevitable clutter of medieval buildings in the Old Town, Warsaw would have acquired one of the most magnificent palatial residences of the period of Classicism in Europe.

Plans for the parliamentary rooms

All of the plans for the rebuilding of the Castle envisaged change in the design of the parliamentary rooms. A design of particular interest was the one presented by Victor Louis at the beginning of the reign of Stanislaus Augustus; he suggested an extraordinarily grand, monumental entrance through a peristyle in place of the Sigismund Tower and then one flight of stairs to the first floor leading to the vestibule area and from there to the two Chambers. The Chamber of Deputies was to be in the west wing and the Senatorial Chamber in a newly-constructed wing on the Kitchen Courtyard. The Senatorial Chamber was to be of an oval shape and its form, the position of the throne and the senators' chairs completely broke with centuries-long tradition. The room was to be surrounded by a colonnade with 24 columns, supporting a gallery with a balustrade. Between the columns statues were to be placed. The interior was to be covered with an enormous dome decorated with a coffered ceiling. The throne was to be placed opposite the entrance at a shorter elliptical angle, at an elevation of three steps and under a canopy in accordance with tradition; on the sides of the throne the senators' seats were to be arranged in a semi-circle, the form of which was connected with the ancient representational method of seating. Behind the senators' seats two rows of benches for the deputies were to be placed, also in a semi-circle. Parliamentary ceremonial used since the time of the Jagiellonians had forced the deputies to stand in the Senatorial Chamber. We are now seeing for the first time in this architectural design the introduction of a new parliamentary custom which permitted the deputies to occupy seats in the presence of the king and senators. It can therefore be said that at the beginning of his reign Stanislaus Augustus not only intended to give a new artistic expression to the parliamentary rooms but at the same time to transform the old Polish Seym into a modern parliament. Attention should also be drawn to the fact that Louis' design for the Polish Seym is the first attempt in the history of architecture to create a functional interior for a modern parliament.

Szreger and other royal architects also drew up plans to alter the parliamentary rooms but none of these plans were actually put into effect. The architectural arrangement in the two chambers of the time of Augustus III remained. It was in these rooms that between 1788 and 1792 the debates of the Great Seym took place which made attempts to reform the anachronistic system of government in the Commonwealth and which went down in history as the creator of the famous Third of May Constitution. The moment of voting for the new constitution by the three estates in the Senatorial Chamber was recorded in several drawings by one of the participants in these events, Jean Pierre Norblin.

The king's private apartments

The rebuilding and decoration of the royal apartments were carried out in several stages. The earliest stage is represented by Louis' designs which were forwarded in 1766 from Paris and gradually carried out on the site. The famous decorator Prieur worked with Louis and designed many sumptuous parts of the interior decoration, e.g. candlesticks, clocks, furniture, picture-frames, etc., either made in Paris or in Warsaw by local craftsmen. Many of these items have been preserved till modern times. Louis and Prieur designed four rooms: the Throne

Room, the Portrait Room, the Bedroom and the Boudoir. These interior furnishings lasted just about ten years. The only trace of them remaining, apart from a few fragments of decoration used during the following rebuilding, are beautiful watercolours kept in the Royal Library of Drawings which now belongs to the Warsaw University Library.

Between 1774 and 1777 a new royal apartment was built, according to the design of Domenico Merlini, which started at the Grand Staircase and Guards' Room, also called the Mier Hall (rebuilt in 1767 by Jakub Fontana) and arranged *en suite* extended to the southeast wing. The Room of Views decorated with a series of views of Warsaw by Bernardo Bellotto-Canaletto, hence known also as the Canaletto Room, served the function of a grand ante-chamber. Nearby was the Royal Chapel decorated with marble-like stucco and covered with a coffered dome, and after the Room of Views came the beautiful Audience Chamber with a ceiling by Bacciarelli showing an allegory of the blooming of art, learning, agriculture, and commerce under the rule of Peace. Then came the Bedroom decorated with rosewood panelling, and beyond it the King's Dressing Room and Study, filled with numerous bibelots and works of art.

These interiors remained more or less the same until 1939. The contents of the rooms and their artistic arrangement will be discussed in more detail in Part III.

The Grand Suite

At the time of the rebuilding of the private rooms the Grand Suite was also constructed which consisted of reception rooms in the main block on the Vistula side. In 1771 under the supervision of Fontana the former Marble Room underwent changes, the marble wall coverings being partly altered and the old portraits of the "Jagiellonian family" being changed into a chronological sequence of likenesses of the kings of Poland from Boleslaus the Brave to Stanislaus Augustus. These portraits were painted by Bacciarelli and the ceiling (with an allegory of Poland) by Jan Bogumił Plersch. The new decorations and the new conceptual design of the Marble Room greatly impressed contemporaries. On this occasion Adam Naruszewicz composed an ode entitled *On the Marble Room, Newly Decorated With Portraits of the Kings of Poland Commissioned by His Majesty King Stanislaus Augustus.*

The other rooms in the Grand Suite were finished in the 1780's, according to the designs of Domenico Merlini and Jan Chrystian Kamsetzer and aided by the painters Bacciarelli and Plersch and the sculptors Le Brun and Monaldi. The most magnificent interior was that of the large two-storey Assembly Hall with walls divided by pillars and decorated with mirrors. The most impressive room was the Knights' Hall which contained large paintings of scenes from Polish history, portraits and busts of famous Poles, and monumental statues representing Chronos, the God of Time, and a winged Fame. This room was therefore a kind of Pantheon dedicated to the memory of early national deeds and heroes and at the same time an illustrative lesson of past greatness.

The Conference Room was a tiny masterpiece of architecture and decoration with gilded walls covered by Plersch with subdued grotesque ornamentation which provided a background for seven portraits of European monarchs who ruled at the same time as Stanislaus Augustus.

The Royal Library

Of the buildings constructed in the second half of the 18th century mention is due also to the Royal Library which was designed by Domenico Merlini between 1780 and 1784 in the north wing of the Tin-Roof Palace (*Pałac Pod Blachą*). The library room was extended to 56 m in length and was given a beautiful architectural shape. It was divided by pairs of marble columns into three parts. In gallery recesses and between the windows were 12 cupboards made from alder wood in a gold-yellow colour and in the middle of the room stood three tables made from the same wood. Under the ceiling a kind of frieze composed of 28 oval bas-relief medallions with personifications of various spheres of knowledge and skills ran around the room. The bas-reliefs were made of white stucco on a yellow marble-like background and represented personifications of Architecture, Music, Painting, Theatre, Optics, Chemistry, Astronomy, Philosophy, Cartography, etc. Between the pairs of columns stood marble busts and in the middle of the room a large seated statue of Voltaire, which was a copy of the famous sculpture by Jean Antoine Houdon. The colour scheme of the room was particularly grand in which the whiteness of the walls contrasted splendidly with the gold-yellow tone of the alder furniture, the books bound in leather with gold lettering on the spines, and the stucco medallions. In the 19th century the book collection and movable furnishings in the library suffered dispersal. The Royal Library is the only castle building which was saved in 1944 and its interior retains a completely preserved architectural decoration of the time of Stanislaus Augustus.

THE CASTLE DURING THE PERIOD OF PARTITION

After the collapse of the Kościuszko Insurrection in the autumn of 1794 and the third partition in 1795, Warsaw was incorporated to Prussia. The only work undertaken on the Royal Castle at that time was to paint black the silver eagles on the canopy in the Throne Room. Frederick William III and his wife Louise, who was famous for her beauty, visited Warsaw three times — in 1798, 1802, and 1805 — and held balls for the Polish gentry at the Castle. During the whole of this period, the nephew of the last king, Prince Joseph Poniatowski, resided at the Tin-Roof Palace. At this time the royal apartments were still in the same condition as Stanislaus Augustus had left them. Countess von Voss, who accompanied the Prussian king and queen in 1798, wrote in her memoirs that "the Castle is particularly large and exceptionally well furnished". At the end of the Prussian occupation many of the furnishings were stolen by Prussian officials. In contemporary inventories we often find a note in the margin saying that something "disappeared after the Prussian withdrawal".

The creation of the Duchy of Warsaw in 1807 changed

the situation of the Castle which became the residence of a constitutional sovereign and the seat of the Polish Seym. Frederick Augustus, King of Saxony, became Duke of Warsaw. He had in fact been named King of Poland by the Third of May Constitution in 1791. The new sovereign often journeyed to Warsaw where he left behind him good memories. However, no artistic or construction work was undertaken at the Castle at this time. The Castle rooms were only filled with many items of furniture and bronze in the fashionable empire style. From this period comes a suite of furniture made by the famous Paris carpenter Pierre Brion and many candelabra, clocks, and decorative vases made in the workshop of Pierre Philippe Thomire. A large number of these items have been preserved in the Castle collection until the present day.

All part of the legendary history of Warsaw is the short visit to the Castle made by Napoleon I. The Emperor of the French, anticipating the great preparations which had been made to welcome him, arrived at the Castle without fuss at night. On his second day in the city, 20 December 1806, the *Gazeta Warszawska* wrote that, "the hero of two centuries, the law-giver of nations, the scourge of oppressors, and the wonder of the entire world, Napoleon the Great, journeying quietly on horseback, has occupied the rooms prepared for him in the Warsaw Castle. The first to welcome him there in solemn silence were the kings of Poland adorning the walls of the Marble Room ..."

The cult and hope which in Poland was connected with the person of Napoleon I and his political ideas within the framework of which an independent and united Polish state was to be reborn found its expression in the design for a monument which was to be erected in the Senatorial Chamber. This idea arose in 1812 when the French forces were bound for Moscow. The Seym of the Duchy of Warsaw under the chairmanship of Adam Kazimierz Czartoryski demanded "the restoration of all her rights to Poland" and asked the support of the Emperor for the national aspirations. Napoleon replied that "I have loved your nation for sixteen years. On the fields of Italy and Spain I saw your soldiers standing by mine. I praise all of their deeds". The Seym decided to inscribe these words on a tablet of Carrara marble and give it a monumental shape. The design was drawn up by the Warsaw architect Piotr Aigner and the tablet was to be placed in the gallery opposite the throne, held on both sides by "life-size Greek caryatids", supporting an architrave and moulding surmounted by shields with the Polish eagle, the Lithuanian coat-of-arms, and the imperial golden eagle.

It was decided to commission the caryatids for the monument from the famous Danish sculptor, Bertel Thorwaldsen, in Rome. Thus, there was the desire to add artistic merit to an enterprise of a political nature. At the end of 1813 the plaster models of the caryatids were ready but before the sculptor could reforge them in marble the political situation all over Europe was different from how it had looked the year before. The Emperor of the French could not now show his good intentions in relation to Poland and there was no one to buy the marble caryatids. Eventually they were purchased by the Danish court and placed on both sides of the royal throne in Christiansborg palace in Copenhagen where they were destroyed by fire in 1884. Of the monument designed for the Senatorial Chamber only the plaster models remained in the Thorwaldsen Museum in Copenhagen.

The Kingdom of Poland was brought into being at the Congress of Vienna in 1815 and was joined to the Russian Empire by personal union with Tsar Alexander I as the constitutional monarch of Poland. Minor repairs were carried out in the Castle at that time and at the end of 1817 and the beginning of 1818 the Chamber of Deputies was renovated and a public gallery supported by Doric columns was erected in the Senatorial Chamber for the opening of the first session of the Seym in the new kingdom. In 1818 the former Large Chapel was transformed into an Orthodox church. At this time the Cracow Gate and the buildings on the courtyard in front of it were burned down, thus creating an irregular square on this site in front of the Castle. The court architect at this time was Jakub Kubicki, the former architect of Stanislaus Augustus. Parliamentary sessions took place at the Castle but the royal rooms were usually empty because the new sovereign rarely came to Warsaw. The Castle came back to life for a short time when the coronation ceremony of Tsar Nicholas I as King of Poland took place in 1829 in the Senatorial Chamber. However, the rule of Nicholas I in the constitutional Kingdom of Poland did not last long. On 29 November 1830 the November Insurrection broke out and the revolutionary Seym of the Kingdom of Poland dethroned Nicholas and the house of Romanov. Patriotic demonstrations took place on the square in front of the Royal Castle.

After the collapse of the insurrection the whole country was subjected to fierce repression from which not even the Castle escaped. The former royal residence was downgraded to the role of governor's residence and the rebuilt parliamentary rooms and Royal Library were turned into barracks. The marble wall covering was removed from the Marble Room and the portraits of the kings of Poland were transferred to St. Petersburg. In addition what was left of the gallery of Stanislaus Augustus and all paintings and sculptures which had subjects connected with Poland's past were taken away to Moscow and St. Petersburg. The paintings of scholars and writers, who took part in the "learned dinners" with Stanislaus Augustus, which were painted by Ludwik Marteau, were burned on the orders of Tsar Nicholas. Several dozen other pictures suffered a similar fate and Houdon's sculpture of Voltaire was broken up.

A rebuilding of the interior was undertaken in the second half of the 19th century but had very little artistic merit. Between 1851 and 1853 the south and west elevations were rebuilt in a late neo-classical style according to a plan by Kubicki which had been worked out in the 1830's.

THE CASTLE AFTER THE RECOVERY OF INDEPENDENCE

After the recovery of independence in 1918 the Castle became a palatial building and after 1926 the permanent residence of the President of the Republic. However the parliament of the new Polish state met in a building on Wiejska Street. The president lived in the Castle where he carried out his official duties, appointed the chairman of the Council of Ministers, the higher state officials, and university professors, conferred decorations, received letters of credence from representatives of foreign states, and gave banquets and receptions. On New Year's Day there was always a colourful ceremony in the Castle for the presentation of new year greetings by the diplomatic corps, the government, and various Polish delegations.

Some rooms were set aside for accommodation for prominent writers. Between 1921 and 1925 Stefan Żeromski lived on the second floor in the Vistula wing where he wrote a number of works including *The Wind from the Sea*. In the north wing of the Tin-Roof Palace another writer, Stanisław Przybyszewski, was given a six-room suite. Often various societies of a cultural or artistic nature met in the Castle, including such institutions as the Society of the Friends of the Reduta theatre which worked towards a development, of the theatre company under the outstanding actor and stage director Juliusz Osterwa, the Polish Pen-Club, etc.

While the First World War was still going on, a series of conservation projects was carried out in the Castle on the instigation of the Warsaw Society for the Protection of Historical Monuments. The Royal Chapel in the Castle Tower was renovated and survey drawings of various interior details were made. The latter were saved during the Nazi occupation and have proved useful during the present rebuilding. Major conservation work was undertaken in 1920 under the supervision of Kazimierz Skórewicz. The greatest achievement was the discovery of the completely preserved Gothic elevation of the Large House and the disclosure of vaulted rooms on the ground floor which housed the Chamber of Deputies in the 16th and 17th centuries. Both were found in 1921 under layers of later plasterwork. Between 1924 and 1927 the pillar decorations of 1851 were removed from the Castle elevations which regained their early Baroque style from the time of the Vasas, and a new roof covered with Dutch tiles was made. In 1928 Adolf Szyszko-Bohusz became the director of conservation work on the Castle and held this post until 1939. His ideas were not always suited to the historical nature of the building. The Grodzka Tower was rebuilt according to his design and increased by one storey on which there was a terrace with a balustrade and on the top of the Tower was the president's flag. From this terrace a bugle call was supposed to ring out to the tune of the *Varsovienne*. In the 1930's the Tin-Roof Palace was renovated and a series of outbuildings, mainly from the 19th century, which disfigured the Castle, were taken down.

For the whole of this period a careful restoration of the historical interiors was carried out. On the basis of a treaty concluded in Riga, the Soviet government returned all pictures, sculptures, furniture, furnishings, and historical objects which had been taken away from the Castle by the tsarist authorities at various times, including the famous Jagiellonian tapestries. It was not possible to recreate in their entirety the Knights' Hall, the Throne Room, the Conference Room, the original Audience Chamber, and the Canaletto Room. Now the former private rooms of the king and the Grand Suite acquired the same appearance they had had at the time of Stanisłaus Augustus. The historical interior furnishings were supplemented by the works of art collected by the Department of the National Art Collections which was founded in 1922 under the supervision of Mieczysław Treter (until 1928) and Alfred Lauterbach (until 1937). Of the newly acquired items the royal insignia of Stanislaus Augustus, two paintings by Jan Matejko, "Báthory at Pskov" an "Rejtan", the illuminated prayer-book of Queen Bona from the 15th century, an oriental carpet from the 16th century (the so-called Wilanów carpet), and a collection of gobelin tapestries from the 16th to 18th centuries were of particular value. An urn with the heart of Tadeusz Kościuszko which had been brought from the Polish Museum in Rapperswil (Switzerland) was placed in the Royal Chapel. However not everything could be done within the short space of twenty years. Work still went on on the recreation of the Senatorial Chamber, the Marble Room, and a number of other historical interiors, when Germany invaded Poland on 1 September 1939.

THE DESTRUCTION AND
REBUILDING OF THE CASTLE

The outbreak of war, the siege of Warsaw, and the first months of the German occupation were a short but dramatic period in the history of the Castle, a period of unparalleled destruction to the historic building and of attempts to save it by Polish conservation experts and art historians. On the day of the outbreak of war the staff of the Castle started to protect the most valuable works of art. The two Matejko pictures and the most valuable gobelin tapestries were taken down and rolled up. On 5 September the civil chancellery of the president was evacuated and the staff took with them the Matejko paintings, the tapestries with the coat-of-arms of Dymitri Chalecki and the royal insignia of Stanislaus Augustus. Kazimierz Brokl was left as Castle custodian and responsibility for the cultural treasures collected here devolved upon him. When a corner of the Castle was struck by the first artillery fire on 8 September, Brokl took the urn with the heart of Kościuszko to the vaults of St. John's Cathedral.

On 17 September 1939 the Castle became the object of mass shelling which resulted in the burning of the roofs and cupolas of the Sigismund and Ladislaus Towers. At the same time St. John's Cathedral was set on fire. In the memoirs of the people who took part in the rescue operation this day is referred to as "Black Sunday". The fire in the Castle came to the knowledge of the mayor of Warsaw, Stefan Starzyński, who sent teams from the Municipal Department of Architecture there under the supervision of Wilhelm Henneberg. Eleven divisions of the fire brigade led by Captain Zbigniew Borowy, took part in putting out the fire. The fire-fighting was extraordinarily difficult as constant bombardment caused new sources of flames. However, they succeeded in preventing the conflagration from spreading to the whole building, which was helped by the fire-proof roof fitted in the interwar period.

The campaign to save the works of art was led by Brokl with the help of Jadwiga Przeworska from the Ministry of Religious Creeds and Public Education and Marian

Słonecki, curator of the Castle collections. They were assisted by the Castle staff, the inhabitants of the neighbouring houses, soldiers from the units stationed in the environs of the Castle, and members of the Citizen's Defence. One of the participants in the campaign, at that time a corporal in the Machine Gun Battalion, Leon Borkowski, remembers that, "in the large hall there was smoke and fire. We tore down curtains from the windows and then... we took down large pictures from the east wall on the Vistula side. We shuffled pictures over the parquet floor to the north side of the Castle which had not yet caught fire... I remember very well civilians running, carrying the smaller pictures and busts from the room". Teams from the National Museum were also involved in rescuing the Castle collections. "That day I was at the Castle with Professor Walicki," writes Stefan Kozakiewicz in his memoirs. "Our teams had the task of transporting the most valuable works of art from the threatened residence while people and the staff of the Castle helped the fire brigade to put out the fire... We started pulling the net curtains down from the windows and wrapping historical ceramic objects in them, beginning with some Italian Renaissance majolica... We returned to the Museum by lorry along Krakowskie Przedmieście and Nowy Świat streets under artillery fire." On this day Kazimierz Brokl died while on duty, hit by a shell splinter. The fire brigade did not succeed in putting out the fire on the roof of the Assembly Room. The large Bacciarelli ceiling representig "The Dissolution of Chaos" was completely destroyed. The moment of putting out the fire in the Assembly Room was captured for posterity by the photographer Henryk Śmigacz and the burning Sigismund Tower was photographed by the American cameraman Julien Bryan who was in Warsaw at that time and who took his rolls of film with him from the beleaguered city.

The bombardment of the Castle continued for the rest of September but not on such a mass scale. The collections assembled here could not remain in a devastated building without a roof or window panes, with gates and doors wrenched off by the force of exploding shells. The National Museum, the Municipal Administration, and the

Museum Department in the Ministry of Religious Creeds and Public Education engaged in a campaign to protect the collections. They were led by Stanislaw Lorentz, the director of the National Museum, who was helped by Michał Walicki, Jan Morawiński, Stefan Kozakiewicz, Maria Friedel-Bogucka, Zygmunt Miechowski and Jadwiga Przeworska from the Ministry (who was murdered by the Nazis in the Ghetto in 1942), and Kazimierz Skórewicz, the first curator of the Castle, already retired at that time. Students from the Officers' Training Corps also helped and even railwaymen from Silesia and boy scouts from Brodnica whom the war had brought to Warsaw and hundreds of other people who cannot be identified today. Under the extraordinarily difficult conditions of a city under siege, with no transport available, during the course of continuous bombardment and artillery fire, many pictures, sculptures, pieces of furniture, tapestries, and other works of art were transported to the Museum. This campaign lasted until the capitulation of Warsaw on 28 September. For the wole of this period the standard of the President of the Republic, a red flag with a white eagle surrounded with a general's braiding, flew from the Grodzka Tower. It was taken down the day after capitulation on the instigation of Jadwiga Radlińska, the daughter of the former custodian Brokl, who was living in the Castle at that time. "It was quite obvious to me that at the moment the German forces entered Warsaw, the standard would immediately be ripped down by them. A man who worked at the Białowieża Residence who happened to be on the Castle site at the end of September took it down. Unfortunately I don't remember his name now. I stood at the Castle Gate and watched the last fluttering of the standard... It was completely undamaged — neither the fire nor the shelling had touched it. It was rolled up by the man, who took it with him and promised to hide it... I had the satisfaction of not having it touched by German hands." These are the memories of Mrs. Radlińska.

After the cease-fire and the German entry into the capital the building could still basically be quickly rebuilt in spite of the burned roof and partial devastation. This was stated by a commission composed of architects and art historians under the chairmanship of Marian Lalewicz, the president of the Society for the Protection of Historical Monuments. The Municipal Administration started to bring in building materials and began work on protecting the wing on the Vistula side which housed the most valuable historical interiors. However right at the beginning of October the German occupation authorities began a systematic looting of the Castle contents and around 20 October forbade any repair work whatsoever. On 10 October Hans Frank, the Nazi Governor of occupied Poland, came to inspect the Castle and tore down the silver eagles and the canopy over the throne and incited the Nazis accompanying him to do likewise.

The appearance of the Castle at this time has been described by one of the staff of the Castle Administration, Eugeniusz S. Osikowski: "Everywhere damage done by the fire and shelling was apparent. The Sigismund and Ladislaus Towers damaged, stripped of their cupolas, the reinforced concrete of the roofing partly laid bare, the window frames empty, and both courtyards (the main and the kitchen ones) covered with rubble and various fittings destroyed during bombardments and lootings. German police were stationed at the Grodzka, Clock, and St. John's Gates. In the Grand Courtyard there were several lorries into which terrorized Jews, who had been rounded up, were loading looted Castle contents — furniture, carpets, tapestries, pictures, etc... All in all a shocking picture of destruction, devastation, and plundering."

At the end of October units of German sappers took over the Castle and began to bore holes in the walls to put explosives in them to blow up the Castle. On news of this, Polish conservation experts and art historians, thinking that the decision was a misunderstanding, protested to the German occupation authorities and even threatened to inform Berlin. The reply was given that the decision had in fact been made in Berlin. It was not yet known that Hitler himself had made the decision and that Frank had written in his diary, "the Fuehrer... has approved... the destruction of the Royal Castle in Warsaw and the decision not to rebuild the city". Soon it became clear that the Germans were bent on the complete annihilation of the historical building. Construction teams brought in by them began to dismantle historical parts of the interior decoration — panelling, flooring, fire-places, and other architectural details, and also technical equipment like central heating installations, fireproof ceilings, and anything which could serve as building material. The dismantling was directed by the German scholars Dr Dagobert Frey, Professor Gustav Barthel, Dr Josef Muehlmann and Dr Kurt Muehlmann. At a secret meeting of the Society for the Protection of Historical Monuments under the chairmanship of Marian Lalewicz, Polish art historians, architects, and conservation experts decided to save everything they could of the Castle interiors from the barbaric activities of the Germans. They undertook this work because everyone knew that one day in the future the Castle would have to be rebuilt and fragments saved of the architectural structure would be an indispensable help in the work of reconstruction. This task was entrusted to the director of the National Museum, Stanisław Lorenz, who was helped in his work by the Municipal Administration.

The German authorities agreed that parts which had not been taken away by Frey and Muehlmann could be stored in the National Museum. Polish teams started work on the Castle at the beginning of November. Those who took part were Bohdan Marconi, Jan Morawiński, Zygmunt Miechowski, Józef Grein, Stanisław Gebethner, Stanisław Pawłowski, Bohdan Guerquin, Maria Friedlówna, Stanisław Jankowski, Jan Łukasik, Włodzimierz Życzkowski, Zofia Jełowiecka, Antoni Wieczorkiewicz and the distinguished Castle curator, Kazimierz Skórewicz, for whom the work of dismantling a building to which he had devoted great efforts to return it to its original artistic style must have been a particularly hard task. The Polish teams worked under very difficult conditions with the constant terror of the police, in an unheated and devasted building. In addition the winter was early and severe that year: "The temperature reached -27°C and terrible things were happening in the Castle. Some Germans were boring holes in walls in which they were placing explosives. Others were taking up the parquet flooring and the wall coverings. They forced Jews to take down the ceiling beams, beating them as they did so in the most cruel way. The Castle resounded to the shouts of Germans, the cries of those being beaten, and the din of those pulling down the walls and ceilings... all the time we were working under surveillance and every step threatened us with death. We were not allowed to move from room to room." These are the reminiscences of Stanisław Jankowski, the stucco expert, who together with his two sons worked for several days removing pieces of stucco. Stanisław Jankowski Jun. adds that "the cold was biting. Our hands went numb and today I am amazed that we were able to do anything at all but in fact we worked from morning to evening".

In December 1939 the occupation authorities removed all Polish teams from the site of the Castle. They began to pull down ceilings in the denuded building and by doing so destroyed the few remaining decorations. Thus the beautiful Bacciarelli ceiling was destroyed in the former Audience Chamber which the Germans did not allow the Polish conservation experts to take away. The work on devastating the Castle had come to an end. Out of a building which two months before — in spite of the fire on 17 September — had been one of the most magnificent residences in Europe only bare walls remained. However, explosives had not yet been placed in the several thousand holes bored into the walls by Wehrmacht sappers. Still today we do not know why the decision was taken not to blow up the Castle after all at the end of 1939. Perhaps regard for the opinion of neutral countries prevailed where Polish diplomatic missions had shown pictures of the barbaric devastation of the Castle.

These pictures were taken and then transported through Hungary and Italy by Adam Moraczewski who handed them over to the Polish government-in-exile. The bare walls of the Castle lasted until the collapse of the Warsaw Uprising in October 1944. When the fighting ceased dynamite was placed in the holes which had been made five years earlier. Warsaw was a dead city at this time and thus today we do not know when the Castle was reduced to a pile of rubble, whether it was at the end of October or in December 1944. The former inhabitants of

Warsaw returned to the liberated city in January 1945 and were able to read on a miraculously preserved cartouche, fixed to a fragment lying on top of the ruins of the wall, the motto of the Order of the White Eagle — *Pro Fide, Lege, et Grege.*

The destruction of the Castle was only apparent however. Only the walls have been blown up. In the Warsaw National Museum hundreds of works of art which used to be part of the decoration of the rooms and hundreds of architectural details had been preserved. Straight after the war an enormous number of pieces of panelling, door wings, fireplaces, sculpture, and pictures which had been scattered by the Nazis was found. Some were in Cracow in the boiler room of the university Library, or in the Wawel Castle, where Frank had established his headquarters, others were in the depths of Germany or in Austria. In 1947 the rubble on the site of the Castle was cleared and a large number of stone fragments from the elevations put up under the Vasa and the Saxon dynasties were found. Only the building of the Royal Library and the north wing of the Tin-Roof Palace had survived intact. In addition the scorched walls of the latter palace, the lower storeys of the Grodzka Tower, and some fragments of walls and the cellars remained. In the same year the portal of the Grodzka Gate was erected from fragments which had been saved. At the beginning preparatory work on the rebuilding of the Castle was carried out in the Department for the Rebuilding of the Capital and then in the Conservation Department of the Capital. The director of the works department, called the Stanislaus Department, was Jan Dąbrowski. On 2 July 1949 the Legislative Seym passed a decree, summoning the government to undertake the rebuilding of the Castle "to make it the seat of the supreme authority of People's Poland and a centre of cultural life for the broad mass of the people". However, the final decision to rebuild the Castle was postponed several times. Voices arose questioning the feasibility of the decision to rebuild a historical monument which had been completely destroyed. However, the necessity to rebuild the Castle was widely understood, above all because it was a symbol of Polish culture and sovereignty.

Stanisław Lorentz argued the point that almost all the furnishings and most of the historical interiors had been saved or found and a large amount of the external stone-work had been discovered among the rubble.

The period of dispute and discussion ended on 20 January 1971 when Edward Gierek, the First Secretary of the Central Committee of the Polish United Workers' Party, in front of a group of cultural and academic experts, announced the decision of the Central Committee to undertake an early reconstruction of the Castle, "this symbol of our national culture which Nazism tried to destroy and which has been reborn and flourishes in People's Poland".

This view met with widespread approval in all sections of society and found its expression in newspaper columns in Poland and among Polish communities abroad and the spontaneous donation of money and works of art and valuables. By the early hours of the next day — 21 January — Stanisław Kochanowicz had informed the editors of the weekly magazine *Stolica* that he would give 500 zloty to the rebuilding of the Castle. The same day the illustrious actress Mieczysława Ćwiklińska handed over 10,000 zloty with the same aim. A year later the Rebuilding Fund amounted to 125,635,889 zloty. In reply to a poll carried out by the Polish Press Agency as to whether people thought the rebuilding of the Castle was a good thing, 86.1 per cent of those asked said "Yes".

On 26 January 1971 the Citizens' Committee for the Rebuilding of the Royal Castle was set up. The chairman was Józef Kępa, the then First Secretary of the Voivodship Committe of the Polish United Workers' Party, and the vice-chairmen were Professor Stanisław Lorentz, the director of the National Museum, Jerzy Majewski, the mayor of Warsaw, and Janusz Wieczorek, the chairman of the Council for the Protection of Monuments of Struggle and Martyrdom and head of the Office of the Council of Ministers. Scholars, artists and representatives of various social groups and professions were appointed as members of the Committee. The Committee set up various boards — for Architecture, for Research, for Architectural Conservation, for the Rebuilding Fund, and for Publicity. A department was set up as the executive organ of the Citizens' Committee which was changed into the Department for the Reconstruction of the Royal Castle in 1975. Carrying out the work was entrusted to the Monument Conservation Workshops.

The Board for Research has substantial control over all of the work on conservation, construction, archaeology, and museum collections, and the Board for Architectural Conservation approves all the projects to be carried out.

Over the next few years, day by day and month by month, the walls of the Castle arose. The building site was constantly surrounded by crowds of onlookers. Thousands of Varsovians and people from all over Poland did several million zlotys worth of voluntary work. University professors, famous specialists in various fields, specialized academic institutes, places of work, and also those who could only do the simplest work, contributed their knowledge and skill without remuneration. Schools, offices, military units, and various organizations and associations gave their help. Just to mention all their names would increase the size of this book to a hefty volume. However, their hard work and good will will not be forgotten. The work on rebuilding the Castle has not yet been finished, the generosity continues, and money keeps flowing into the Citizens' Committee's bank account. When the rebuilding work is finished, it will be necessary to publish a separate book recalling the contribution of the entire nation and the efforts of all Poles, and the extraordinary phenomenon of a unified society and national emotion, and the attachment to historical tradition and cultural heritage.

However let us now recall some basic facts from recent past. In February 1973 the building of the walls of the south-east wing (the former Gothic Large House) was finished and the traditional topping-out ceremony took place. At the same time work was going on on the south, west, and north wings. By spring 1974 the main block of the Castle was ready; on 29 June of the same year copper cupolas were placed on the corner towers and on 6 July one was placed on the Sigismund Tower. This latter operation was carried out with great efficiency and observed by crowds of Varsovians in Castle Square. A solemn ceremony took place on 19 July, when in the presence of Henryk Jabłoński, the Chairman of the Council of State, the Citizens' Committee for the Rebuilding of the Castle, and enormous crowds, at the symbolic hour of 11.15 a.m., the hands of the clock on the Sigismund Tower, which had stopped on "Black Sunday" in 1939, started moving again.

In 1974 the second stage of the rebuilding began involving more arduous and detailed work on the Castle interiors. Parquet flooring, plasterwork, coloured stucco work, and panelling were recreated in the private suite of Stanislaus Augustus, covering the Grand Staircase, the Mier Hall, the Officers' Room, the Canaletto Room, the Royal Chapel, the former Audience Chamber, the King's Dressing Room, and the King's Study. In all of these rooms fragments of the architectural decoration which had been preserved were used. At the same time the Jagiellonian Rooms, the former Chamber of Deputies, and the rooms on the ground floor of the south wing were restored to their original appearance. A meeting of the Citizens' Committee took place on 26 January 1977 in the recreated Audience Chamber in which only the Bacciarelli ceiling, furniture, and pictures were missing.

The next stage in the recreation of the artistic interiors of the Castle will cover the Royal Grand Suite and other historical rooms. Interest in the rebuilding and the generosity of the population have still not slackened. At the time of going to press the bank account of the Citizens' Committee stood at over 810,000,000 zloty and over 750,000 dollars and the number of voluntary hours worked amounts to over 310,000; on the list of donations of historical objects and works of art there are 1,566 items recorded. The Royal Castle in Warsaw has been rebuilt by the will, effort, and hard work of the entire Polish nation.

PART III

PART III

THE CASTLE REBUILT

THE LAYOUT OF THE CITY AROUND THE CASTLE AND CASTLE SQUARE

The present urban layout and surroundings of the Castle are the result of numerous changes which took place in this area in the 19th and 20th centuries. The most picturesque view of the Castle is from what is known as the Royal Route, i.e. Krakowskie Przedmieście, which is a show piece in Warsaw today. The Castle was erected within the medieval defence walls which now stop on the west side of the present Castle Square but which formerly cut across the square diagonally and reached the Grodzka Tower. At the entrance to Senatorska Street the medieval Cracow Gate was erected through which traffic passed to the town and to the Castle. Along the wall, perpendicular to the Castle façade, were various service buildings, the royal kitchens, the stables, the coach houses, etc., covering the area of the present Castle Square which in the 17th and 18th centuries had the aspect of a front courtyard. The defence wall and the service buildings separated Krakowskie Przedmieście from the Castle buildings and the area of the Old Town. The buildings in front of the Castle were of one storey and therefore hid the lower floor of the Castle façade, the silhouette of which with its three towers could only be seen over the roofs of the low service buildings.

In the Middle Ages there was a moat along the walls over which a stone bridge situated in front of the Cracow Gate was built. After the middle of the 17th century the moat was filled in and over the next few centuries many houses were built here. The bridge too was covered in and thanks to this it has been preserved in almost perfect condition until today and was unearthed during the course of excavation work in 1977.

In 1643 and 1644 a column with a statue of King Sigismund III on it was erected in Krakowskie Przedmieście or more exactly in a small square which existed at that time in front of the Cracow Gate, on the instigation of Ladislaus IV. In 1694 the Cracow Gate became a palatial façade on the Krakowskie Przedmieście side with a central projection broken up by pillars in a long sequence and topped with a triangular gable filled with a cartouche with the arms of King John III held by two mermaids. The Cracow Gate or rather its sumptuous façade together with the column of Sigismund III created a picturesque closure to the view up Krakowskie Przedmieście. On the east side of the street, where today there is a stone balustrade with an underpass below and from where there is a broad view down the East-West Thoroughfare and the Mariensztat district, stood St. Clare's Church and a Bernardine convent. Along the opposite side since medieval times there have been burgher houses which were rebuilt several times in the 18th and 19th centuries.

The stretch of Krakowskie Przedmieście from St. Anne's Church and the Bernardine monastery to the Cracow Gate served as the main square in Warsaw from the 16th to the 18th centuries. In front of the Cracow Gate the city council solemnly welcomed the king after his coronation and presented him with the symbolic keys to the city. In front of St. Anne's Church the kings of Poland accepted homage from the princes whose lands belonged to the Polish crown. Such ceremony took place for the first time on 26 February 1578 when King Stephen Báthory handed over the Prussian principality to Margrave George Frederick of Ansbach of the house of Hohenzollern. This way came the processions of the fiefs of the Polish crown — the princes of Courland, Moldavia, Wallachia, Lębork and Bytów in Pomerania, and the processions of delegates from foreign courts. A magnificent procession took place here in 1596 when the special papal legate, Cardinal Enrico Gaetani, came to Warsaw. Near St. Anne's Church the city council built triumphal gates on the occasion of royal visits or when a hetman made a triumphal entry into the city after a victorious campaign, bearing spoils and bringing prisoners. A magnificent triumphal gate was built in 1677 when King John III Sobieski returned to Warsaw after his victory over the Turks at Żurawno. What these triumphal gates looked like and how these "entries" into the city took place can be seen in the picture of Johann Samuel Mock who showed the welcome given King Augustus III after his coronation in 1734 by the city council. Finally this was also the route from the Castle to the Holy Cross Church followed by King Stanislaus Augustus, the Seym, and the Senate in solemn procession on the first anniversary of the Third of May Constitution in 1792.

The urban layout described above was completely altered in the 19th century. Between 1808 and 1818 the Cracow Gate and all of the buildings on the Front Courtyard were pulled down and the area was occupied by an irregular triangular place. One of the sides of the place was made by the Castle which was irregularly positioned in relation to the start of Krakowskie Przedmieście, and another by the burgher houses erected along Przedzamkowa Street which no longer exists. The Sigismund Column was now in a large open space and together with the Castle tower became the main vertical accent in the new square. This solution, connected with the picturesque and irregular urban layout of the age of Romanticism, was certainly not a favourable one and was completely at variance with the original Baroque idea. However, the Castle and the Sigismund Column in front of it remained alive in the consciousness of the people as an inseparable fragment of the landscape of old Warsaw.

In 1842 St. Clare's Church and convent were pulled down to make a road in their place and to permit an approach to the viaduct and bridge across the Vistula. The viaduct was built by the engineer Feliks Pancer between 1844 and 1846 and improved city communication but contributed unfavourably to the appearance of the Square and Castle.

During the 19th century Castle Square was often the scene of patriotic rallies and revolutionary demonstrations directed against the partitioning powers. In December 1830 a demonstration by the people of Warsaw took place here in support of the decision of the Revolutionary Seym of the Kingdom of Poland, thus showing the insurrection against tsarist rule to be a popular one, and in January 1831 the people cheered on the occasion of the deposition of the house of Romanov carried by the Seym and showed their admiration of the Russian Decembrists. During the January Insurrection bloody demonstrations and clashes between the people and Cossack troops took place here. On 8 April 1861 over a hundred people were killed by the firing on a defenceless crowd. People talked about these events all over Europe and illustrations showing the massacre on Castle Square appeared in leading newspapers in many countries.

During the interwar period Castle Square was tidied up and resurfaced with granite and created a suitable entrance to the residence of the President of the Polish Republic in the Royal Castle. After the collapse of the Warsaw Uprising in 1944 all of the surrounding area of the Castle with the exception of St. Anne's Church was set on fire and burned down. A German tank fired at the Sigismund Column with a heavy calibre gun and the monument was shot down as it were.

The rebuilding of this part of the city was carried out between 1948 and 1958. The former viaduct designed by Pancer was taken down and in its place the modern East-West Thoroughfare was laid out with an underpass running under Castle Square which was finished in 1949. The same year the Sigismund Column was erected, its shattered shaft being changed for a new one made from Silesian granite. In 1958 the historical burgher houses were rebuilt on the west side of the Square and in 1971 reconstruction of the Royal Castle was begun.

The Castle from the South

On the south side the Castle is built on the edge of a gorge which cuts across an escarpment. In the Middle Ages a small river called the Kamionka ran along the bottom of the gorge. The building of the East-West Thoroughfare very much brought the previous layout of this area into relief. The south wing of the Castle is connected with the Grodzka Tower, the lower floor of which dates from the 14th century. The medieval part of this building has bricks left unplastered in a Gothic manner. Adjoining the tower is a rectangular building covered by a copula-style dome with a lantern, which houses the presbytery of the Castle chapel dating from the 16th century. The tower is three storeys high but in the Middle Ages it must have been much higher because it was then called the Great Tower (*Turris Magna*). Its present form is a reconstruction carried out in 1974 on the basis of iconographic records from the 17th and 18th centuries.

In the middle of the south wing is the Castle Gate with a stone portal, which leads to the Grand Courtyard. This portal is completely composed of original fragments which were found after the Castle had been blown up and which in 1947 were fixed into a preserved part of the south wing.

Below the Grodzka Tower on the east side is the Tin-roof Palace, so called in the 18th century because of its hitherto unheard of roof covering of copper sheeting. The main body of the Palace was erected at the end of the 17th century and between 1720 and 1730 side wings which encompassed a courtyard were built and a late-Baroque façade was added to the main part. In 1777 Stanislaus Augustus joined the Palace to the complex of Castle buildings and between 1779 and 1784 the architect Domenico Merlini constructed the building of the Royal Library along a side wing of the Palace. The Palace was the residence of Stanislaus Augustus' nephew, Prince Joseph Poniatowski, commander-in-chief of the Polish army during the Duchy of Warsaw and Marshal of France, at the beginning of the 19th century. In 1944 the Palace was burned down and rebuilt in 1948—49. A side wing of the Palace and the Royal Library were the only Castle buildings of which the walls and some of the interior decorations were saved in 1944.

The Castle from the West

If we stand in Castle Square, the best places being where the city walls end or where Piwna Street starts, the formidable façade of the Castle stretches out in front of us with its tall five-storey Sigismund Tower, topped with a copper cupola with a pinnacle, surmounted with a standard with the Polish eagle under a gold crown on it. In the Tower is a gate enclosed by a rusticated portal which is the main entrance to the Grand Courtyard. The west wing with the Tower and the two corner turrets was completed in the second decade of the 17th century. In 1619 a cupola was added to the Tower and in 1622 a large clock, with golden hands and numbers and two bells, made in Gdańsk by Gerhardt Benninck was fixed to it. The clock mechanism was made by the clockmaker Gerardo Priami who was specially brought in from Florence. The façade and the Sigismund Tower remained in only a slightly changed state until recent times. The corner turrets were lost in 1704 and not reconstructed. On 17 September 1939, when the German artillery shelled the Castle, the cupola of the Sigismund Tower and part of the roof was set on fire. The clock mechanism was destroyed, the bells fell down, and the hands of the clock stopped at 11.15. In 1944 this whole part of the Castle was reduced to rubble. It was rebuilt in 1974 in accordance with what it looked like before the destruction and at the same time the side turrets were recreated on the basis of early iconographic records. Many fragments of the stone window frames which were discovered in the rubble were mounted in the new wall, together with the corner rustications and the portal.

The Castle from the North and the Kitchen Courtyard

The north wing of the Castle pentagon is situated in the triangular Kitchen Courtyard. The elevation of the north wing, similar to the façade and elevation of the south side, has stylistic features of the early Baroque period. Situated in the middle of the building is the Senatorial Gate enclosed by a rusticated portal, largely reconstructed. The north wing was built around 1604, completely destroyed in 1944, and rebuilt in 1974.

The name of the Courtyard comes from the building of the royal kitchen which was once situated here. The first townhouse opposite the Castle elevation, situated on the corner of the Courtyard and Świętojańska Street, was given in 1433 by Princess Anne of Mazovia to the priests of St. John's Church and it is called *Mansjonaria* (the Priests' House). According to tradition the Duke of Mazovia, Janusz III, died in this house in 1526. The next, modern building which houses the Department for the Reconstruction of the Royal Castle, was erected in 1970 according to the design of Jan Bogusławski. In the same spot the royal kitchens were erected in 1738 according to the design by Gaetano Chiaveri and pulled down in 1843, and replaced by an administrative building with no real style. A small alley is joined to the Courtyard along which runs the east wing, composed of several buildings adjoining each other. The two storey house with four windows on each floor was built in 1969 (design by Jan Bogusławski) in place of the former court painting studio which was run by Marcello Bacciarelli at the end of the 18th century and where many Polish painters were trained. The building, which owes its architecture to the forms of the 18th century, is nevertheless a completely modern composition, and it houses the "Wedding Palace". The next one storey building was used as the royal kitchen in the 17th century and the following one is a former palace where Queen Anna the Jagiellonian resided at the end of the 16th century. The way now leads through a vaulted gate to the Castle gardens. All of these buildings conceal medieval remains in their walls, many of which were discovered between 1950 and 1960 during the examination of the ruins. In the Middle Ages the whole area was covered by a residential complex called the Lesser Court (*Curia Minor*). On the opposite side of the alley is a side wing of the mansion of the dean of the Collegiate Church (St. John's). The front elevation is visible from a small courtyard which can be reached through a gate. The originally Gothic dean's court was rebuilt in 1610 and given a modest early Baroque form. It now houses the Secretariat of the Polish Episcopate.

The end of the alley is enclosed by a gate which was called the Cemetery Gate in the 16th century because on the small square beyond it was a cemetery. Later it came to be called the Canon's Gate. Over the arch of the Gate is a passage, a kind of concealed gallery, which leads from the Castle to the royal pew in St. John's Church. This gallery has existed since the second half of the 16th century and in those days only linked the church with the residence of Anna the Jagiellonian. The gate and gallery acquired their present architectural form at the beginning of the 17th century. Although burned down in 1944 they were rebuilt immediately after the war. After passing through the Canon's Gate another "flying gallery" is visible, thrown across Dziekania Street and linked directly with the church.

St. John's Cathedral
and the royal pew

The cathedral is the oldest church in Warsaw, erected in the 14th century as a parish church, raised to the rank of a Collegiate Church in 1406 and a cathedral in 1797. It is a Gothic hall church with two aisles and finished off with an extended multilateral presbytery. During the Uprising in 1944 the Cathedral suffered complete destruction. The Germans launched attacks into the interior of the church with the help of tanks. Only the walls of the presbytery were preserved. The church was rebuilt between 1948 and 1956 under the supervision of Jan Zachwatowicz. The interior of the church today is almost empty. The former royal pew was situated on the right hand side of the presbytery. It originally had rich, Baroque decoration which was changed into Neo-Gothic between 1836 and 1840. During the last rebuilding only the recess for it was left in the wall and its former function is indicated by a stained glass window with the Polish eagle situated above.

St. John's Church was the scene of many historical events. The sessions of the Seym always began here with a solemn service. Several royal coronations took place here — those of Queen Cecilia Renata in 1637, Queen Eleonora Maria Wiśniowiecka in 1670, Stanislaus and Catherine Leszczyński in 1704 and Stanislaus Augustus Poniatowski in 1764. In 1791 the Seym, Senate, and King, in the presence of an innumerable crowd of people, sang the hymn of thanksgiving *Te Deum Laudamus* in this church after the passing of the Third of May Constitution.

The Castle from the East and the Castle garden

Returning to the area of the Castle through the Canon's Gate and then through the so-called Terrace Gate we come to the garden, situated on the steep slope of the escarpment. Here the rear elevations of the buildings of the east wing can be seen with their fragments of Gothic brick walls. An Italian style garden with geometrically arranged flower beds and pruned plants was founded here in the middle of the 16th century by Queen Bona and later looked after by Anna the Jagiellonian. In the course of the following centuries the garden went through several alterations. In the 17th century exotic trees in large pots were placed on the edge of the escarpment and a small garden with six flower-beds was established on the flat triangular area by the south-east wing. There were sculptures, fountains, and even ornamental bird-cages. In 1650 Queen Marie-Louise founded a botanical garden here which acquired some fame as Simon Paulli wrote about it in his book *Viridaria varia regia et academia publica...*, published in Copenhagen in 1653. The book mentions that there were 737 species of plants in the Castle garden. This can be compared with the royal garden in Paris which had 2,121 and the Oxford University garden which had 1,472. The Castle garden was also described by the court botanist Jan Kazimierz Marcin Bernitz. In 1737 Gaetano Chiaveri designed a new garden of a French Baroque type, with regularly shaped flower beds spread out on the slope of the escarpment. In the 19th century the garden was transformed into a romantic landscape design with luxuriant flora which hid the architecture of the Castle elevations on the Vistula side in an unsuitable way. It remained in this style until modern times and now work is going on to recreate the garden in style appropriate for the 18th century.

The most monumental and remarkable building from an artistic point of view, visible from the garden side, is the main body of the Castle which was erected between 1741 and 1746 according to the design of Gaetano Chiaveri and altered by Zacharias Longuelune. The main block has three projections strongly thrust forward, the middle one with seven sides and rounded corners and the two side ones square with three sides with windows. Between the middle projection and the side ones there are cloistered galleries supporting terraces. The elevation is adorned with lavish sculptural decoration by Jan Jerzy Plersch. The parapet of the middle projection bears a foundation stone and over it a cartouche with the coat-of-arms of the Commonwealth under the royal crown enclosed by panoplies. On both sides of the stone are two female statues which symbolize Poland and Lithuania and decorations composed of war trophies. The triangular gables of the side projections are filled with medallions with the initials of Augustus III and Queen Maria Josepha, supported by winged mythological figures. These decorations symbolize the triumph of the Commonwealth under the rule of Augustus III. The elevations are French Neo-classical architecture of the 18th century and the fantastic and irregular sculptural decoration displays rococo characteristics. This elevation is one of the most innovative and excellent works of Polish architecture.

This section of the Castle buildings was destroyed in 1944. Only the corner of the left projection and a fragment of the tympanum remained. This fragment made it possible to restore the real scale and height of the building during reconstruction. Now it has been built up and connected with new walls. The sculptural decoration is to a large extent the original one as many fragments were found amid the ruins.

The Grand Courtyard

From the Castle gardens we return through the Terrace Gate and the Kitchen Courtyard to the Senatorial Gate which leads to the Grand Courtyard. The courtyard, built according to a pentagonal design, was constructed in the first decade of the 17th century when three new wings —

the north, west, and south — were added to the existing buildings on the east side.

The oldest building, from the beginning of the 15th century, is the Large House which now composes the south-east wing of the Castle pentagon. The Gothic elevation of the Large House, broken up by a series of ogival blind windows, was uncovered between 1920 and 1924 by Kazimierz Skórewicz. This elevation is a complete reconstruction. Another building was built on to the Large House at an obtuse angle and at the point where it joins it an octagonal tower was erected called the Ladislaus Tower. This building and the tower are the remains of the Royal House which was built between 1569 and 1572 by Giovanni Battista Quadro for Sigismund Augustus. The architectural design of the tower, the portal and its cupola date from 1600-4. From the 16th century to 1746 the main grand staircase to the royal apartments was here. The stone portal surmounted by a large cartouche with the Polish Eagle surrounded by the chain of the Order of the Golden Fleece is partly composed of the original fragments saved in 1939 or discovered amidst the ruins later. The buiding beyond the former Royal House was constructed between 1600 and 1604 as another part of the royal rooms. The design of the elevation also dates from this period.

The elevation of the north wing was originally Early Baroque. It was rebuilt between 1740 and 1742 when it acquired its present appearance. The designer of the new elevation was Antoni Solari. The portal of the Senatorial Gate dates from the first half of the 17th century. Many parts of it, including the large beams supporting the balcony, are composed of the original pieces.

The elevation of the west wing, with the Sigismund Tower in the middle, was preserved until recent times and was given its original Early Baroque style by Giovanni Trevano. The garret of the Tower, which formerly was the home of the clock-master who looked after and repaired the Castle clock, was built in the second half of the 17th century. The Early Baroque portal of the gate and the door portal to the Deputies' Staircase were partly reconstructed in 1977.

The elevation of the south wing owes its style to the

elevation of the north wing opposite it. It was designed in 1767 by Jakub Fontana. The sculptured panoplies on the top of the projection, the portal of the Castle Gate, and the corbels supporting the balcony which runs along the entire elevation are almost completely the original ones.

The Grand Courtyard was the scene of many colourful court celebrations, exciting ceremonies, entertainments, and galas. Here by the stairs in the Ladislaus Tower came the carriages of the foreign diplomats or the senators and ministers of the two nations, who were successful in obtaining an audience with the king. Along the courtyard stood guard detachments in their colourful uniforms made in the Hungarian style, who presented arms to the visitors. The band played a fanfare. The Royal Chamberlain welcomed the ambassadors of foreign courts at the stairs and the Grand Marshal came to meet them in the first room. In 1635, on the occasion of the signing of the peace treaty with Muscovy, a firework display took place in the Courtyard which Giovanni Battista Tartoglini, the private secretary to the ambassador of the Grand Duchy of Tuscany, who was present at the time, described with admiration. The wedding celebrations of the marriage of King Ladislaus IV with the Archduchess Cecilia Renata provided also the occasion for various court festivities including the fights between wild animals — bears against bison set upon by dogs. The spectators watched the scene from the Castle windows. In 1641 a ceremony of homage took place in the Courtyard, paid to Ladislaus IV by Frederick William, the Elector of Brandenburg. On a raised platform covered with red cloth and positioned opposite to the gate in the Ladislaus Tower, the king sat surrounded by the senators. Behind the royal throne stood the Royal Standard-Bearer with the Prussian standard of feifdom and the Sword-Bearer holding a sword. The Elector rode on horseback into the Courtyard through the Senatorial Gate. He dismounted opposite the throne, bowed three times to the king, went up to the platform, and prostrated himself on the steps of the throne. Then, kneeling, he delivered a long speech "in Latin in a good accent" — so wrote with admiration Prince Stanisław Albrycht Radziwiłł, Grand Chancellor of

Lithuania, who was present during the ceremony. He then swore loyalty to the Polish crown and received the standard of feifdom from the hands of the king. During the reign of Augustus III many festivities took place here; around the Courtyard tables covered with all kinds of food were set up and wine flowed from the barrels on which figures of Bacchus sat. All the gentry present in Warsaw took part in these banquets.

In interwar Poland various state ceremonies usually started in the Grand Courtyard and then continued in the Castle rooms, like the arrival of representatives of foreign states to present their letters of credence to the President, or other official visits to the Castle. Ceremonies taking place here affected the whole nation. One of them was the funeral of the writer Stefan Żeromski who died at the Castle on 20 November 1925. After the mournful ceremony in the Assembly Hall the coffin was placed in the Grand Courtyard where President Stanisław Wojcie-chowski, the Speakers of the Seym and the Senate, Maciej Rataj and Wojciech Trąmpczyński, Prime Minister Aleksander Skrzyński, and crowds of Varsovians paid homage to the great writer. In addition ceremonies took place here which vividly recalled a distant era and the ceremonial of monarchs in the Baroque period. In January 1927 the papal ablegate, Monsignore Chiarlo, brought a cardinal's hat to Poland for the papal nuncio in the country. There existed a custom dating back to medieval times that the kings of Poland handed over cardinal's hats to the nuncios, a role later taken over by the President of the Republic. The presentation of the hat to the papal nuncio, Lauri, by President Ignacy Mościcki took place at the Castle with extraordinary pomp with the participation of state dignitaries, the diplomatic corps, and the clergy. On the Grand Courtyard military detachments presented arms when the three coaches surrounded by a squadron of the First Light Cavalry Regiment arrived through the gate in the Sigismund Tower, preceded by four buglers on white horses; in the first coach was the ablegate's secretary and the President's A.D.C.; in the second, the ablegate, dressed in a red gown and ermine, accompanied by Count Petrucci, the captain of the papal guard; and in the third Nuncio Lauri and Stefan Przeździecki, the chief of diplomatic protocol. They were greeted at the Town Gate and fanfares were played from the balcony. The President waited for the nuncio and the ablegate in the Knights' Hall. A ceremony like this had not been seen in Poland since 1784.

THE INTERIORS

The Jagiellonian Rooms

The main entrance to the Castle rooms is now through the Senatorial Gate and a large vaulted hall was designed here from scratch. In the 18th century, this part of the Castle contained the Exchequer of the Commonwealth where the money of the royal treasury was kept in locked chests. From the hall a modern staircase leads to the subterranean level which is taken up with cloakrooms, public conveniences, cafés, and rooms for temporary exhibitions.

The first suite of historical rooms is on the ground floor of the north-east wing which has absorbed the former Royal House of Sigismund Augustus. For this reason this suite is called the Jagiellonian Rooms. However the arrangement of the first four rooms dates from 1600-4. The vaulting in the first room, kept in the style of an entrance hall, and in the next was made at the same time. In the two other rooms were flat bare ceilings in the 18th century and vaulting was only built here in the 1930's and has now been reconstructed. The remaining rooms — a long vaulted room and two other rooms on the Courtyard side — are within the walls of the Royal House of Sigismund Augustus from 1569—72. The vaulting, which in the old arrangement had a Renaissance style, very similar to the vaulting done by Giovanni Battista Quadro and Giacomo Pario in the other buildings constructed by them, is now of a free composition and only recalls the historical original. Beneath these last three rooms in the subterranean level is a large hall with cross vaulting divided into four parts supported on one central pillar. This interior is all that remains of the building work between 1569 and 1572 which was relatively well preserved after the blowing up of the Castle in 1944. Originally this hall was not a cellar but the ground floor or mezzanine which is indicated by the preserved window recesses. Probably the guards' room was here.

All the Jagiellonian Rooms are adorned with period furniture, fabrics, pictures, and ceramics from the 16th century. The tapestries are worthy of attention and include "The Building of the Tower of Babel" from the series "The Tragedy of the Jewish People", made in 1572 on the basis of a cartoon by Maarten van Heemskerck (1498—1574), the Dutch painter and lithographer, and six tapestries which make up the series "The Life of Pompey", made in the second half of the 16th century in Brussels in the weaving studio of Franz Geubels. Also worthy of attention are the portraits of the Jagiellonians — Sigismund the Old, Bona Sforza, Isabella the Jagiellonian Queen of Hungary, Anna the Jagiellonian, and her husband Stephen Báthory (these portraits were a gift from the government of the Federal Republic of Germany) and also the portrait of Queen Barbara Radziwiłł, the beloved wife of Sigismund Augustus.

A romantic story is linked with the name of Barbara Radziwiłł in the Castle. Sigismund Augustus married Barbara secretly and, in defiance of his mother Queen Bona, and the entire public opinion of that time, crowned her in Cracow in 1551. Shortly after the coronation Barbara died, plunging the king into deep mourning. 18 years later, on a January night in 1569, a strange event took place which may have been enacted in one of the rooms described above. Here before the king, lost in yearning for his beloved Barbara, the sorcerer Twardowski called forth the spirit of the dead queen. Later historical research has shown that this Twardowski was certainly the same as the famous Nuremberg magician, Lorenz Dhur, and the entire supernatural happening was skilfully staged by the court clique. At least the story of the romance between Sigismund Augustus and Barbara Radziwiłł has passed into the legend of literature and in the 19th century, during the period of Romanticism, it was a subject dealt with frequently by Polish writers and artists.

The next suite of rooms is housed in the oldest building in the Castle, the medieval Large House. From 1570 these rooms were used by the Seym. The first large hall with vaulting supported on one pillar served as the parliamentary chancellery. Now here hang the portraits of the Mazovian dukes of the 16th century — Konrad (III) the Red-Haired, the joint portrait of Stanisław, Janusz and Anna, and a portrait of Zofia Odrowąż, the daughter of Princess Anna. A valuable work of art is the tapestry called "David and Bathsheba", made in Brussels around 1520 in the studio of Michael Moer, according to the cartoon by Jan van Roome.

After the parliamentary chancellery comes the former Chamber of Deputies. Originally this was a long, vaulted room, divided by a row of six columns into two parts. Now there are two separate rooms here with their vaulting supported on three and two pillars respectively. The former furnishings consisted of the deputies' benches, the Speaker's chair and a table and chairs for the secretary and staff who wrote down the decrees. The benches were positioned only on the left side of the room and in the central area was the Speaker's seat and the secretary's table. The right side was empty, intended for the public, who listened to the debates while standing. The spatial arrangement of this room was designed by Quadro but the present architectural structure dates from the early 17th century when the columns were thicker and octagonal in shape, and the form of the vaulting was changed to a kind with four intersecting divisions. The rebuilding was designed by Giovanni Trevano.

After the Chamber of Deputies was transferred to the first floor in the west wing this room lost its original function. In the 18th century it was divided by walls into a series of smaller rooms which were intended for the office of the court treasurer and later for the royal chancellery. The vaulting however remained unchanged and the former pillars remained in the partition walls. Thanks to this Kazimierz Skórewicz was able to restore the room to its former architectural shape after pulling down the partition walls. For unknown reasons the wall dividing the Chamber of Deputies into two rooms was not taken down. During the latest rebuilding this arrangement was retained, which has a very unsuitable effect on the artistic expression of the entire layout of the room.

At the moment the first part of the Chamber of Deputies is decorated with portraits of Polish and Luthuanian dignitaries of the 17th century and the second part with portraits of the kings from the house of Vasa. Among the portraits of the dignitaries the most interesting ones are the beautiful portrait of Jerzy Ossoliński (painted by Bartłomiej Strobel) who was the Speaker of the Seym between 1631 and 1635, the portrait of Stanisław Krasiński, the voivode of the Płock region (painted by Daniel Schultz), and also the portraits of Stefan Pac, the Speaker in 1629, and Leon Sapieha, the Speaker in 1637. There is also a sumptuous Flemish tapestry from the end of the 16th century with a scene of a lion hunt and the coat-of-arms of Dymitri Chalecki, who was the Speaker of the Chamber of Deputies in 1589.

All the Seyms used to debate in this room until the 1670's. Here, at the first convocation during the interregnum in January 1573, the legal basis for the government of the Commonwealth was worked out and it was decided that from then onwards the throne of Poland should be an elective one and the power of the king should be circumscribed by laws. During the same year a decree was ratified which testifies to the political maturity of the country and contemporary Polish parliamentary activities. This decree went down in history as "the act of the Warsaw confederation" and guaranteed religious peace to the country and equal rights to dissenters. "...We jointly promise to preserve peace among ourselves both for our own advantage and that of our descendants and not to shed blood for different beliefs..." ran the wording of this decree. It is worth remembering here that the same year a few months earlier the terrible St. Bartholomew's Massacre had taken place in France and the principle of *cuius regio, eius religio* was generally in force. Many less savoury matters however went on in the Chamber of Deputies with much futile discussion and squabbling between various cliques, and finally in 1652 under the chairmanship of Andrzej Maksymilian Fredro the principle of unanimity for the passing of decrees was sanctioned, known as the *liberum veto*, which led to the downfall of Polish parliamentarism. However, scandalous events and anarchy were more the exception than the rule and always met with general condemnation, even among those who had aroused the anarchy. Magnificent speeches were sometimes made in the Chamber of Deputies which aroused the interest of Europe and illustrious statesmen led the debates. It was loud and colourful here as the room was filled with a mass of deputies and arbitrators who looked just like the portraits now hanging on the walls.

The next two rooms, situated in the south wing, made up one large "entrance hall to the Chamber of Deputies" in the 17th century and played the role of a guard's room (Marshal's Hungarians). This rooms is now decorated with furniture, tapestries, and portraits from the 17th century.

The private apartments of Stanislaus Augustus

From the guards' room the Grand Staircase leads to the first floor. The Staircase was built at the beginning of the 17th century according to the design by Trevano. The stucco decoration on the arch-bands of the vaulting on the landings date from the 1720's and the classicized panels, festoons and rosettes were designed in 1768 by Jakub Fontana. The Grand Staircase facilitated communication between the Chamber of Deputies on the ground floor and the Senatorial Chamber of the first floor. During the reign of Stanislaus Augustus it was used as a grand entrance to the private apartments of the king. The apartments of Stanislaus Augustus are made up of a suite of rooms of the highest artistic level, and, apart from the Łazienki Palace-on-the-Island, constitute the only complex of this kind in Poland. The rooms were built between 1774 and 1777 according to the design of Domenico Merlini and Jan Chrystian Kamsetzer. The first room is the guards' room which is also called the Mier *(Mirowska)* Hall (the name comes from the surname of Wilhelm Mier, the commander of the royal guard which was on duty here). The decoration of the walls which are broken up by pillars and shallow galleries was designed by Jakub Fontana in 1768. The nature of the room as a guards' room is emphasized by the stucco overdoors with figures of cherubs playing with pieces of military equipment. Over the doors opposite the entrance is the only original overdoor, all of the other are reconstructions. Some fragments of the original stucco work — the capital of a pillar and some rosettes — have been fitted into the wall decoration.

Next to the Guards' Room is the Officers' Room which was assigned to the officers on duty. On the walls are four large paintings, ordered by Stanislaus Augustus from Paris in 1767 and originally intended for the Grand Antechamber in the reception suite but never in fact made use of there. The scenes depicted in these paintings were chosen by the king and were supposed to symbolize the ideas of magnanimity, justice, noble rivalry and harmony. The pictures show "The Moderation of Scipio" (painted by Joseph Marie Vien) with magnanimity symbolized by the act of Publius Scipio the Elder who after the capture of Carthage returned to the defeated commander his beautiful financée without ransom; "Caesar's Fear on Viewing the Head of Pompey" (painted by Jean Louis François Lagrenée) in which justice is exemplified by an epilogue of the struggle between Julius Caesar and Pompey when the latter was treacherously murdered by Theodotus, the governor of Egypt, and Caesar is shown the head of the murdered man and shudders at this shameful deed; "Julius Caesar Before a Statue of Alexander the Great" (painted by Vien) shows a scene from Caesar's stay in Cadiz where he is supposed to have expressed regret while standing in front of a statue of Alexander the Great that he had not attained the same glory as Alexander had at his age; "Scylurus, King of the Scythians, Ordering His Sons to Agree" (painted by Nöel Hallé) is an illustration of the famous legend about the Scythian king and his sons whom he ordered to break a single arrow and then a whole quiver of them as an example of strength in unity.

The next room — called the Room of Views in the 18th century and later the Canaletto Room — served as an ante-room for the Audience Chamber. The walls are completely covered with a series of 24 paintings by Bernardo Bellotto, known as Canaletto, with views of Warsaw. The artist started painting these pictures before 1770 and finished in 1778. Apart from these there is also a large canvas by the same painter representing the election of Stanislaus Augustus in 1764 (the painting was made in 1778) in which we see what was known as "the shed" where the Senate debated, a circle of deputies, the crowds of gentry and the Primate Władysław Łubieński, who went round the election field in a carriage collecting the votes. All of these pictures, like the fragments of panelling and the fireplace of white marble, were saved during the war. The beautiful parquet floor made from several kinds of wood is a reconstruction which was made according to prewar measurements.

Next to this room is the Royal Chapel which is one of the loveliest rooms in the so-called Stanislaus Augustus style. The Chapel is housed in the Grodzka Tower. It is composed of two parts — a nave and a sanctuary with an altar, made in the form of a circle and covered with a coffered dome. The walls of the sanctuary are covered with marble-style stucco in brownish red and columns made of green stucco. The capitals and bases of the columns, the rosettes in the dome, and the dove in the rays symbolizing the Holy Spirit have been gilded. Six of the eight columns and the capitals were removed from the Castle before it was blown up and have now been replaced in their original positions. Part of the rays around the dove are also the original pieces. The altar as it existed at the time of Stanislaus Augustus was destroyed in the 19th century. There now hangs in the Chapel a picture representing "The Madonna and Child" which was executed in the studio of Rubens; nearby on pedestal stands an urn with the heart of Tadeusz Kościuszko in it.

The former Audience Chamber contains part of the former Senatorial Chamber, which was housed here between 1570 and 1740. The walls of this room are covered with red damask edged with gold braid and large wall mirrors. Opposite the entrance is a throne under a canopy. This canopy was reconstructed on the basis of earlier designs. The ceiling is being reconstructed by a team of artists under the direction of Janusz Strzałecki. On the basis of preserved measurements the ingenious parquet flooring has been recreated out of several kinds of wood with a large "revolving" rosette in the middle. On the other hand, part of the original furnishings of the room which were saved during the war are the four pictures by Bacciarelli which are hung as overdoors and symbolize the cardinal virtues — Courage, Wisdom, Piety and Justice. The four gilded corbels and the throne were in this room at the time of Stanislaus Augustus, as was the bronze appliqué work on the walls and the candelabra of gilded bronze which were made in the second half of the 18th century by the famous Paris firm of bronze-smiths, Etienne Maurice Falconet. The fireplace set consisting of a vase and two censers made of gilded bronze and imitation porphyry and also a large rotating clock in the shape of a vase, placed on a pedestal, also come from the royal collection. Other examples of the original fittings are large parts of the fireplace, four sculptured eagles on laurel wreaths positioned in the panelling over the mirrors and parts of the carved decoration in the panelling, including the rosettes, festoons and skirting boards.

Before the Grand Suite in the main block was ready, Stanislaus Augustus gave audiences in this room. During the 1780's the function of the room was changed and sittings of the Permanent Council, the highest administrative authority in the Commonwealth at that time, took place here. 24 chairs were added to the existing furnishings, which were covered in red damask and arranged on the sides of the throne along the room. They were used by the senators and deputies who took part in the sittings of the Council.

From here we proceed to the King's Bedroom. It is a smallish room with an alcove, decorated with panelling made of honey-coloured yew wood. The panelling and the wings of the doors are decorated with gilded branches and garlands of laurel leaves. This same motif is repeated in the stucco decoration on the ceiling. The panelling and the door wings which are made of the same wood were taken down and removed from the Castle before its destruction. On the sides of the alcove are two fireplaces of white marble (parts of which are original).

Two paintings by Bacciarelli were also saved and are now positioned on the overdoors; they show "Rebecca and Eleazar" and "Esther and Ahasuerus". The splendid glass chandelier hanging from the ceiling is a gift from the President of Austria, Dr. Rudolf Kirchschlaeger and the suite of tapestry-covered furniture in this room was presented by Princess Alexandra of Great Britain. The walls are covered with reconstructed fabric with a design of small flowers and the canopy over the bed has been made from the same material. This room with its unusually elaborate proportions, decorations, and colour scheme is counted among the most original works of Polish Classicism.

The next two rooms are the King's Dressing Room and the King's Study, linked to each other by a wide passage. Their architectural structure is relatively modest. The walls are covered with smooth green silk and hung thickly with paintings in the manner of the 18th century. In the Dressing Room are mainly canvasses by Dutch, French and Italian painters of the 17th and 18th centuries, some coming from the former gallery of Stanislaus Augustus, while the Study contains paintings by Polish artists or artists who worked at the royal court. Particularly noteworthy are two sketches by Marcello Bacciarelli for the ceiling in the Assembly Hall which show "The Dissolution of Chaos", a sketch by Jan Bogumił Plersch with a design for the ceiling of the Marble Room, pictures by Bernardo Canaletto, Franciszek Smugle-wicz, Kazimierz Wojniakowski, and others. There is also a self-portrait by Bacciarelli who was involved in all the artistic enterprises of Stanislaus Augustus. On the sides of the fireplace hang two splendid portraits of the King's parents — Konstancja Poniatowska, neé Czarto-ryska, with her son Stanisław, who later bacame Stanislaus Augustus (painted by Augustin de Mirys) and Stanisław Poniatowski as castellan of Cracow (painted by Bacciarelli). All of the pictures have elaborate gilded frames, decorated with a cartouche with the initials of Stanislaus Augustus. The pictures in the royal gallery were framed in this way but only a few of the frames have survived to modern times. They are at present being reconstructed on the basis of preserved original examples.

Of the eleborate furniture which was placed here at the end of the 18th century, nothing has survived till today. Only two mahogany book cases come from the former furniture of the Castle and the rest of the furniture, two chests of drawers and two escritoires, inlaid with multi-coloured veneers, made by French cabinet-makers, come from the collection of the National Museum. The desk in the King's Study, signed by David Roentgen, is a gift from Valery Giscard d'Estaing. However, the clocks, candelabra, and decorative faience vases made at the royal workshop in the Belvedere, come from the former Castle collection.

The Study and the Dressing Room made a small private suite for Stanislaus Augustus. Here the king worked, received his trusted staff, had discussions with artists, writers, and scholars, and here the ideas for the cultural and political revival of the country were born. In these modest rooms, surrounded by beautiful works of art, Stanislaus Augustus spent many hours of his difficult reign. Here he once received an unexpected visit about which there was much talk at court and among the citizens of Warsaw. He often used to read lying on a chaise-longue behind a glass-panelled screen through which he could observe the room unseen. On such an occasion it happened that a chimney sweep boy who was cleaning the chimney fell down the rope into the fireplace in the king's Study and to the astonishment of the king came out of the fireplace and began to look around the room. On a small table lay royal orders, studded with diamonds, rings, a watch and other valuables. The sweep, seeing that the room was empty, put all of these jewels on, looked at himself in the mirror, and then took them off, returned them to their original place and disappeared up the chimney. Out of curiosity the king had himself informed as to who had cleaned the chimney and had the boy brought to him. He chatted with him, praised him for his honesty, and gave him a generous reward. The boy was then called the royal chimney sweep. The anecdote, which is certainly genuine, illustrates Stanislaus Augustus' great gentleness and his sense of humour.

There is another anecdote connected with the king's Dressing Room. When Napoleon I stayed for a short time at the Castle in 1806, he ordered the bed from the Bedroom of Stanislaus Augustus to be brought from there and placed in the Study as — the story runs — he did not wish to sleep in the bedroom of a sovereign who lost his throne. The Grand Empereur of the French did not foresee the whims of Fortune.

Next to the royal Dressing Room is a room of a modest architectural form which is called the Second Dressing Room. On the walls hang paintings by artists connected with the court of Stanislaus Augustus. In the corner the original preserved stone fireplace has been fitted. Oak doors lead to the staircase in the Ladislaus Tower, which, from the rebuilding by Quadro in the 16th century to 1741, was the grand entrance to the royal rooms, and the two present-day dressing rooms made up one large room called the Grand Entrance Hall. The Second Dressing Room is connected with a corridor which leads to the Canaletto Room and to the suite of reception rooms, known as the Grand Suite in the 18th century.

It should be emphasized once again that the rooms described above, and in particular the Canaletto Room, the former Audience Chamber, and the Bedroom, are composed of many of the original pieces of the previous decoration, like the panelling, door wings, fireplaces, pictures, furniture, decorative bronzes, etc. Therefore they cannot be treated as reconstructions of their onetime appearance but as rooms which have been recreated in their historical place and only supplemented by some necessary pieces.

The Grand Suite

The present visiting route through the Castle is planned in such a way that we come into the reception rooms from the rear as it were. From the 1740's when the new main block was built on the Vistula side, the main entrance was through the Senatorial Gate, up the staircase designed by Gaetano Chiaveri, into a long gallery, and then to a large Ante-Chamber in front of the present Assembly Hall. This grand passage was suited to the Baroque court ceremonial.

The first two rooms, next to the private apartments, are

called the Green Room and the Yellow Room from the wall coverings as they were in the time of Stanislaus Augustus. The Green Room was used at that time as a small dining room. Around 1808 both rooms were decorated with arabesque style painting, which unfortunately has not been recreated. Now the rooms represent the style of the end of the 18th century. The original fireplaces have been fitted in both rooms. From these rooms we proceed to one of the most splendid rooms in the Castle, the Marble Room.

This room was built between 1640 and 1643 at the instigation of Ladislaus IV. The designer of the architectural layout was Giovanni Battista Gisleni and the 22 royal portraits are the work of Pieter Danckers de Rijn. These portraits show the ancestors of Ladislaus IV from the Vasa, Jagiellonian, and Habsburg dynasties (in old inventories they are referred to as "the Jagiellonian family"). Paintings on the ceiling show the various military victories of Ladislaus IV. This room remained much the same until the reign of Stanislaus Augustus, although in 1655 during the Swedish invasion the ceiling vanished. In 1771 the architect Jakub Fontana changed the interior to a small degree by adding a fireplace with a mirror and over it a cartouche with the coat-of-arms of the Commonwealth supported by statues, sculpted by André Le Brun, symbolizing Peace and Justice. Fontana changed the top part of the marble covering on the walls. Instead of the former portraits, 22 likenesses of Polish kings were placed in this room in chronological order from Boleslaus the Brave to Augustus III and a large portrait of Stanislaus Augustus in coronation robes was hung over the fireplace. These portraits were painted by Bacciarelli and a new ceiling with an allegorical representation of Fame was executed by Plersch. After the collapse of the November Insurrection of 1831 this room was destroyed on the orders of Tsar Nicholas I. The marble covering was torn down from the walls and used for other buildings while the statues symbolizing Peace and Justice were placed in the Castle storeroom and the royal portraits were taken away to St. Petersburg. Only the ceiling painting remained here and that was destroyed in 1939.

The room has been reconstructed according to its state after the alterations of 1771, for which the very detailed plans of the time have been of great help. The marble covering on the walls has been reconstructed and the small fragments which had been saved from the time of Stanislaus Augustus — the foundation stone, a few slabs with the names of the kings of Poland on them, and the tablet placed over the portrait of Stanislaus Augustus with a Latin inscription — have been inserted. Also part of the original furnishings of the rooms are the 22 royal portraits, the portrait of Stanislaus Augustus in coronation robes, the statues of Peace and Justice, and the beautiful console-table made of ebony and bronze.

The Marble Room, dedicated to the memory of the kings of Poland, began the historical trend in the Polish art of the Enlightenment. It was an expression of an increase in interest in the history of the country and the portraits of the successive kings of Poland placed here were intended to visualize the country's long and glorious history. It should be also mentioned that four pictures by French painters which now hang in the Officers' Room were originally intended for the Ante-Chamber which preceded the Marble Room. These pictures had a didactic purpose represented by examples taken from ancient history, which, though not disassociated from certain allusions to the contemporary situation in Poland, were of a universal nature. The concept of the Marble Room, built in 1771, indicates a change in the historical and philosophical ideas of the king who at that time stopped emphasizing ancient themes in the Castle decoration and, in order to put into effect a grand programme of an educational and political nature, began to look for subject matter in Polish history. Therefore the Marble Room became a kind of Pantheon, dedicated to the memory of the kings of Poland and at the same time displaying an allegory of the country's history.

Next to the Marble Room is the Knights' Hall, built between 1781 and 1786, which in a most apposite way displays the didactic and patriotic tendencies of the king's artistic intentions. The room is decorated with six large paintings by Bacciarelli with subjects taken from Polish history, illustrating "Casimir the Great Receiving Pleas from the Peasantry", "The Reopening of the Cracow Academy by Ladislaus Jagiello in 1400", "The Homage of Albrecht Hohenzollern of Prussia in 1525", "The Lublin Union of 1569", "The Signing of the Peace of Chocim with Turkey in 1621", and "The Victory of John III Sobieski at Vienna in 1683".

It is worth remembering that the king chose these events which led to a consolidation in the prosperity of the country and its cultural development or else which, by a wise, peaceful policy and skilful diplomacy, resulted in an increase in the importance of Poland, as illustrated by the homage of Prussia, the Lublin Union, and the Peace of Chocim. There is only one picture here which illustrates a military victory, i.e. that of John III at Vienna. The choice of these subjects on the one hand reflected the king's view of Polish history and on the other hand showed his contemporaries that in the present political situation it was mainly by those kinds of deeds which were presented in Bacciarelli's pictures that it was best possible to contribute to the good of the state. The placing of a picture showing the battle of Vienna in the Knights' Hall resulted from a cult, which Stanislaus Augustus fostered, of John III and at the same time reminded people that as well as wise policies effective military successes also played a part in Polish history.

In addition to paintings based on scenes from Polish history other paintings by Bacciarelli have been placed in this room on the overdoors. They are portraits of famous Poles, commanders, statesmen, and scholars, including the Hetman Jan Karol Chodkiewicz, Cardinal Stanisław Hozjusz, the artillery commander Marcin Kątski, Nicolaus Copernicus, and the historian Marcin Kromer. In the corners of the room are large bronze busts of Jan Zamoyski, Stefan Czarniecki, Paweł Sapieha, and Stanisław Jabłonowski, all sculpted by Le Brun, and a series of eighteen smaller busts around the room including Hevelius, the astronomer, Maciej Kazimierz Sarbiewski and Piotr Kochanowski, the poets, Jeremi Michał Wiśniowiecki, the hetman, Adam Naruszewicz, the historian, and Andrzej Chryzostom Załuski, the chancellor, all sculpted by André Le Brun and Jakub

Monaldi. On the shorter sides of the room are two monumental statues of Chronos, the God of Time, supporting on his shoulders the globe of the world, and a winged Fame, holding a trumpet and a golden garland of laurels. A motif which is repeated in various arrangements in the decoration of the room is the laurel leaf or branch. They are shown on a smooth level in the picture frames and panelling and made into naturalistic branches out of carved and gilded bronze to make wall brackets. A Latin inscription runs around the room, HIC MANUS OB PATRIAM PUGNANDO VULNERA PASSI, QUIQUE SACERDOTES CASTI DUM VITA MANEBAT: QUIQUE PII VATES ET PHOEBO DIGNA LOCUTI INVENTAS AUT QUI VITAM EXCOLUERE PER ARTES: QUIQUE SUI MEMORES ALIOS FECERE MERENDO, which can be translated as: "This assembly [of portraits] represents those who fought for their country and suffered injury, priests whose lives were pure and righteous, those who gave speeches worthy of Apollo, and those who exalted their lives through the arts, and those who became famous during their lifetime."

Stanislaus Augustus decided on the plan of contents for the room after discussion with the historians Adam Naruszewicz and Jan Albertrandi and it was put into effect by the architect Domenico Merlini, the painter Marcello Bacciarelli, and the sculptors André Le Brun and Jakub Monaldi.

The statue of Chronos symbolized transience and the statue of Fame with her trumpet seemed to announce the everlasting honour and glory of all the Poles "who became famous during their lifetime". Therefore just as the Marble Room was dedicated to the apotheosis of the kings of Poland, the predecessors of Stanislaus Augustus on the throne, the Knights' Hall was a pantheon of famous men who in the past had contributed to an increase in the glory and power of the country through their courage, work, or abilities.

One other aspect of the room serves to underline this point. In one of the pictures Casimir the Great, who was called "the peasants' king", is shown at the moment of receiving pleas from the peasantry. This is the first example in Polish art of introducing the representatives of the people as fellow creators of the historical process and participants in the apotheosis of the Commonwealth.

In the complex of the Grand Suite the Knights' Hall performed the function of a waiting room for the Throne Room. This is where the dignitaries waiting for an audience with the king assembled. The likenesses of famous men and the subject matter of the pictures which decorated its walls created a majestic conceptual plan in this room, reminding Poles and foreigners alike of the magnificent past of Poland.

It should also be remembered that all the pictures, portraits, sculptures, and a considerable number of pieces of the stucco work, like the panoplies enclosing the portraits on the overdoors, the door wings, and the panels from the window frames, were saved from destruction during the last war.

The next, unusually lavish room is the Throne Room which was built between 1783 and 1786. The walls are adorned with large mirrors and covered with crimson velvet clasped in richly sculpted frames with rose, leaf, and laurel garland motifs; the panelling, overdoors, and the ceiling edges are decorated with gilded ornamentation made of acanthus stems. All of the door wings were preserved from the previous arrangement of the room and are decorated with bas-relief gilded ornamentation of laurel wreaths, as were the decorated pieces of panelling in the window reveals, parts of the sculpted frames, and pieces of the the stucco work which show bunches of fasces on the edges, and one complete marble fireplace (the other one is a reconstruction). Other examples of the original furnishings are the throne, two consoles with the tops made of mosaic, the bronze wall appliqués, and the four statues of Hannibal, Scipio Africanus, Julius Caesar, and Pompey made in 1785 in Rome by Angelico Puccitelli on the basis of classical sculptures. Unfortunately an unusually valuable console-table made of ebony and gilded bronze which was placed under the mirror opposite the throne vanished during the war as did a rotating clock in the shape of a vase with an allegorical figure of Astronomy and two cherubs supporting a cartouche with the coats-of-arms of the Commonwealth and the Poniatowski family, which was placed on the console.

Only the cherub group and the cartouche were saved from the clock. The clock and the console, both designed by Jean Louis Prieur in 1766, were two of the most valuable items in the Castle. The throne canopy with silver eagles embroidered on it was also destroyed (now reconstructed). The velvet wall-coverings, the parquet floor and the ceiling have all been reconstructed on the basis of previous designs and measurements.

Next to the Throne Room is a small, octagonal Conference Room, the walls of which are decorated with grotesque style painting on a golden background (the work of Jan Bogumił Plersch). There are also seven portraits of rulers who reigned contemporary with Stanislaus Augustus: Pope Pius VI, painted by Pompeo Battoni, the Emperor Joseph II, painted by Josef Hinckl, King Louis XVI of France, painted by Alexander Roslin, King George III of Great Britain, painted by Thomas Gainsborough, King Frederick II of Prussia, painted by Friedrich Lohrmann, the Empress Catherine II of Russia, painted by Antonio Albertrandi and King Gustavus III of Sweden, painted by Per Krafft.

Original pieces include all the portraits of foreign monarchs, the furniture — the four tabourets and small table with a top inlaid with pieces of Sévres porcelain, painted with scenes from the story of Telemachus — four wall consoles, appliqué work, and a considerable part of the arabesque wall painting which was removed in the autumn of 1939. The rest of the wall decoration was reconstructed and the beautiful parquet floor with arabesque motifs is also a piece of reconstruction.

The Conference Room is one of the most impressive and harmoniously composed rooms of the Stanislaus Augustus era. The likenesses of foreign monarchs on the walls were supposed to indicate and define Poland's place among the countries of Europe. Here the king used to hold private councils and receive foreign ambassadors and envoys.

The largest room around which the other rooms in the reception suite are concentrated is the Assembly Room (also called the Ball Room), situated in the middle projection of the main block and adjacent to the Knights'

Hall (described above) on one side and the Council Room on the other. It is preceded by the Large Ante-Chamber. The Assembly Room was built between 1779 and 1783 according to Merlini's design. The main architectural decoration are the double columns made of gilded stucco which enclose a gallery with windows and large mirrors. On the side of the main entrance are two marble statues, sculpted by Le Brun, of Minerva, goddess of Wisdom, and of Apollo, protector of the Muses. Over them in decorated cartouches have been inscribed the mottoes of the Polish orders — *Pro Fide, Lege, et Grege* (for faith, justice, and the nation) which is the motto of the Order of the White Eagle and *Praemiando incitat* (he who wins this [order] encourages), the motto of the Order of St. Stanislaus. Over the door, supported by two statues symbolizing Peace and Justice, is a medallion with a bust of Stanislaus Augustus. The entire composition and the two statues and the double door decorated with bas-relief panoplies were taken down and removed before the destruction of the Castle.

Other original pieces include the two overdoors over the side doors with Polish eagles on oval shields, enclosed by acanthus stems. Among other valuable works of art saved in this room is the set of six large candelabra, made in 1767 in the Paris studio of the bronze-smith, Philipe Caffiéri. The enormous Bacciarelli ceiling entitled "The Dissolution of Chaos" suffered destruction on 17 September 1939 and the present painting is a reconstruction.

Court receptions took place in the Assembly Room. Here in 1806 during the presentation of the ladies of Warsaw to Napoleon he is supposed to have uttered the words which have long been rememberd in Poland: "How many beautiful women there are in Warsaw."

In front of the Assembly Room is the Grand Ante-Chamber which was known as the Báthory Room before the Second World War because of the large painting by Jan Matejko, "Báthory at Pskov", which was placed in the room. Stanislaus Augustus planned pictures by Vien, Hallé, and Lagrenée for this room. It is now the start of a gallery with a series of historical pictures by Jan Matejko.

From here we proceed to the long room which was the Speaker's Dining Room or "second table", where the courtiers sat down for dinner. Before the war Matejko's painting "Rejtan" hung in this room which was the reason why it was known as the "Rejtan Room". This room is now designed more as a passage gallery connected to a new flight of stairs.

From this room a wide doorway leads to the Council Room where various conferences took place with the participation of the king. The room also functioned as a dining room. From 1771 onwards famous writers, poets, scholars, and thinkers gathered here on Thursdays for dinner with Stanislaus Augustus. They included Adam Naruszewicz, Ignacy Krasicki, Stanisław Konarski, Stanisław Trembecki, Franciszek Zabłocki, Grzegorz Piramowicz and Marcin Poczobutt. At these dinners, which were really academic and literary meetings, the reform of the state government was discussed, literary works, plays, and public pamphlets were read, and plans for academic and literary works were undertaken. At one of these "learned dinners" the idea arose to work on a *History of the Polish Nation* which was undertaken by Naruszewicz and published between 1780 and 1786. In this circle of intellectuals, cultural progressives, and patriotic politicians, ideas were born which led to the establishment of the National Theatre, the Society for Elementary Books, the National Education Commission (the first secular ministry for public education in Europe), and finally the famous Constitution which was approved by the Seym on 3 May 1791.

During the period of Stanislaus Augustus the Council Room was covered with red velvet. There was a series of portraits of scholars and writers who took part in the king's Thursday meetings, painted by Ludwik Marteau. The furnishings consisted of "a grand chair" for the king, a long table covered with red damask and 24 chairs. The earlier furnishings unfortunately have not survived to modern times. The portraits were destroyed as early as 1832. The only original piece here is the king's grand chair. The decorations and colour scheme of the room have been recreated as they were in the time of Stanislaus Augustus.

The next room was once the Large Chapel which is now used as a concert room. The church decorations were destroyed in the 19th century when the chapel was turned into an Orthodox church. There were some pillars and panels which divided the walls, made in the 1740's according the design of Zacharias Longuelune, which were preserved until 1939. Now the architecture has been considerably modified.

The Grand Suite ends with this room. During the reign of Stanislaus Augustus, and later during the Duchy of Warsaw, the Congress Kingdom, and the interwar Republic, various court and state receptions and ceremonies took place in this Suite.

The Matejko Gallery
in the former royal children's rooms

In the north wing between the Grand Ante-Chamber and the Senatorial Chamber is a succession of rooms which was where the royal children lived in the 17th century, first the sons of Sigismund III and later Jakub Sobieski. After the rebuilding of the Castle between 1741 and 1746, these rooms were called the first, second, and third Senatorial Ante-rooms. Now they house paintings by Jan Matejko which show scenes from Polish history. These paintings and their subjects are widely known. Let us simply comment on two large canvases since they show events which took place in this very castle in the parliamentary rooms not far from here. The first picture is entitled "Rejtan" and shows the dramatic scene at the Delegation Seym in 1773 under the chairmanship of Adam Poniński when the corrupt Chamber of Deputies accepted the Treaty of Partition. When the deputies with the Speaker, Poniński, at their head, were to proceed to the Senate to "unify the estates" and ratify the ignominious treaty, the delegate for Nowogród, Tadeusz Rejtan, threw himself on the ground at the door of the Chamber of Deputies and blocked his colleagues' progress, shouting, "Kill me, trample me, but don't kill Poland." Matejko chose this very moment for his painting. It is not, however, an historically accurate illustration of an event in the Chamber of Deputies but an allegorical representation of the collapse of Poland and the most important heroes and participants in this historical drama. The king never took part in the debates in the Chamber of Deputies and for this reason Stanislaus Augustus could not have been a direct witness of Rejtan's outburst. There were also never any portraits of the Empress Catherine nor a seat from which the Russian ambassador could observe the parliamentary debates. Szczęsny Potocki who is visible in the foreground was only a 20-year old youth in 1773 and had not yet committed treason for which he gained ill-fame at the end of the existence of the Commonwealth. The only authentic details here are Rejtan lying by the door of the Deputies' Chamber, the astonished Speaker, Poniński, and the dramatic atmosphere of the whole event. However, these historical inaccuracies do not deprive this great work of Matejko's of its force but rather increase it through the allegoric representation of the reason and results of the collapse of Poland.

The second picture, entitled "The Third of May Constitution", shows the moment when, after the adoption of this fundamental decree, all three estates of the Seym proceed from the Castle to St. John's Church to sing the thanksgiving hymn *Te Deum laudamus*. Here Stanislaus Augustus can be seen entering the church and behind him the excited deputies carrying the Speaker, Stanisław Małachowski, on their shoulders. Jan Matejko painted this picture in 1891, a hundred years after the passing of the Third of May Constitution, and, as was mentioned above, gave it to the nation with the intention that it should be hung in the parliamentary room in the Royal Castle in Warsaw after Poland regained her independence. Until 1939 the painting was hung in the Seym building in Wiejska Street and now it has been placed in the Castle in fulfilment of the will of this great artist and patriot.

The parliamentary rooms

The parliamentary rooms are in the west wing and the entrance to them was once through the gate in the

Sigismund Tower, and then up the monumental Deputies' Staircase. The present route for visitors begins with the Senatorial Chamber which has been in this place since the rebuilding by Chiaveri between 1737 and 1746. At that time pieces of the architectural layout — pillars, panelling and cartouches — were transferred from the previous room in the south-east wing and refitted here in the new Senatorial Chamber. Therefore the room has preserved some elements from the original design by Zacharias Longuelune.

The Great, or Four-Year, Seym carried on its debates in this room between 1788 and 1792 and pledged to support the new constitutional laws here on 3 May 1791; also the debates of the Revolutionary Seym of the Kingdom of Poland went on here in 1830—31. After the collapse of the November Insurrection and the end of the autonomy of the Kingdom, the Senatorial Chamber was destroyed and changed into a series of smaller rooms. Now the room has been restored to its appearance at the end of the 18th century. On the longer side of the room is the throne which was here at the time of Stanislaus Augustus, but the canopy and the senatorial seats are reconstructions.

The Senatorial Chamber is preceded by the Room of the Marshal's Guard and two conference rooms. The guards' room is decorated with a picture by Kazimierz Wojniakowski, showing "Swearing in of the Third of May Constitution" in the neighbouring Senatorial Chamber, the furnishings and architectural arrangement of which the artist has presented with perfect fidelity, and also a series of twelve large portraits of patriots who were active in the Great Seym and of co-authors of the Third of May Constitution, including Hugo Kołłątaj, Ignacy Wyssogota-Zakrzewski, the mayor of Warsaw, and Adam Kazimierz Czartoryski, painted by Józef Peszka; Stanisław Kostka Potocki, painted by Józef Grassi; and Prince Joseph Poniatowski in his general's uniform and with the sash of the Order of the White Eagle and the Grand Virtuti Militari Cross, which he won in the war of 1792 waged in defence of the Third of May Constitution, painted by Franciszek Paderewski. All of the portraits in this room were commissioned in 1791 and 1792 by the Warsaw City

Council for one of the halls in the Town Hall where they were kept until 1916 and thence in the National Museum. They have now been hung in the room before the Senatorial Chamber to recall the great work done by the Four Year Seym. Next to the Room of the Marshal's Guard are two chancelleries of modest architectural design from the second half of the 18th century which have been recreated in their former style. Here there are portraits of dignitaries and worthies, and pieces of furniture from the first half of the 18th century.

Passing the vestibule by the gate in the Sigismund Tower and the Deputies' Staircase we come to the former Ante-room of the Chamber of Deputies. This room was planned between 1762 and 1764 by Jakub Fontana but has not been preserved until modern times. It is now divided into three smaller rooms. From here is the entrance to the Chamber of Deputies which was built on this site in the second half of the 17th century. It was rebuilt and extended several times, in 1721, 1762—64, and finally in 1817—18. Its parliamentary function was completely lost after the collapse of the November Insurrection.

In the course of the present rebuilding it has been restored to its state in the second half of the 17th century, i.e. during the reign of John III. The measurements of the room, its height, and wall divisions have all been recreated but the stucco decoration which existed in former times has not been reconstructed.

From the 1680's to the period of the November Insurrection the deputies debated here, all bills were discussed, and plans for the Third of May Constitution were worked out. From here, through a succession of the ante-rooms and halls, the procession of deputies made their way to the Senate "to unite the estates" and adopt or reject new bills. It was by the door which leads into the Chamber that the dramatic scene represented in the painting by Matejko took place when Tadeusz Rejtan blocked the passage of the deputies to the Senate with his own body.

On the second floor is the Treasury where there is an exhibition of regalia, historical mementoes, jewels, and particularly valuable items of artistic handicraft which come from the former Castle collections, and donations and collections of the National Museum. Of particular interest are Queen Bona's prayer book, Stephen Báthory's sapphire ring, a piece from an embroidered tablecloth which belonged to Anna the Jagiellonian, the coronation insignia of Augustus III and Queen Maria Josepha, and the sceptre, ceremonial sword, and chain of the Order of the White Eagle, which belonged to Stanislaus Augustus.

PART IV

THE FORMER CASTLE COLLECTIONS AND RECENT DONATIONS

During various periods various collections of valuables and works of art were assembled and kept in the Castle. However as a result of wars and foreign invasions they suffered destruction and dispersal. In the majority of cases the inventories and illustrations of the Castle vanished too, so that today it is difficult to recreate the rich collections which once adorned the Castle rooms. This applies particularly to the collections of Sigismund III and Ladislaus IV, and later of John III. We only know about particular items and rarely about entire sets of works of art which at various times and in various ways passed into the hands of others and can now be found in Polish and foreign museums. Initiated by Stanislaus Augustus, the present furnishings of the rooms and the Castle collections date back to the second half of the 18th century. Various *objets d'art* or even whole collections were added to the Castle collection between 1920 and 1939 when they were given by the Polish people and state to the State Art Collection of the Royal Castle in Warsaw which was created at that time. However, of particular emotional importance are the various donations presented in recent years by Poles resident in Poland or abroad, and also by official representatives of foreign states. All of these works of art and historical mementoes which are exhibited in the magnificent Castle rooms have created one of the richest museums in Poland. In this way they are in keeping with the ideas expressed in the Appeal by the Citizens' Committee for the Rebuilding of the Royal Castle in Warsaw in seeing the Castle as the pantheon of national culture.

Art collections were first assembled in the Castle by the dukes of Mazovia. In 1494 Duke Janusz III of Ciechanów brought to his brother Konrad (III) the Redhaired in Warsaw various valuables, which were certainly only part of the treasure of their father, Boleslaus IV, and their great-grandfather Janusz (I) the Elder. From the register written in that year we know that they consisted of insignia of princely power, five mitres covered with expensive fur and studded with precious stones, a sword — a symbol of princely, military and legal power — and magnificent gowns of red velvet embroidered with gold and sewn with pearls. Items mentioned separately are pieces of riding equipment — richly embroidered saddles and bridles, covered with gold and silver, and set with pearls and sapphires, and a luxurious whip decorated with pearls. In the ducal treasury there was also a large number of various kinds of jewellery, e.g. lavish buttons, buckles, rings, ornate helmet decorations, clasps, etc., made of large pearls and diamonds, and others decorated with emeralds, rubies, and sapphires. One clasp had a pendant in the form of a pelican. Several bags of unworked stones were also listed.

There was also a large amount of silver cutlery, often gold-plated, ampullae, goblets, spoons, bowls, and jugs, and several reliquaries which in the Middle Ages were not only kept in churches but also were collected in royal and princely treasuries.

Of the treasures owned by the dukes of Mazovia, nothing has survived to modern times. The valuable gifts donated by Janusz I to St. John's Church have been irretrievably lost. Among them were beautifully written and bound books, psalters and missals, and "a thorn from the Saviour's Crown" kept in a valuable gold reliquary. Therefore the modest gold ring decorated with Renaissance ornamentation and a fragment of a silk garment decorated with the motif of heraldic eagles found in 1951 in the tomb of the last dukes of Mazovia, Stanislaus and Janusz, are of great historical importance. Another item which once belonged to the ducal treasury is a gold chain composed of 128 links which Duchess Anna Danuta, the wife of Janusz I, donated to the Jagiellonian University in Cracow, where it is still used today as part of the

Chancellor's insignia. This chain is a splendid example of the goldsmith's art, made in the 5th or 6th century, and therefore a valuable historical piece even at the time when the duchess of Mazovia presented it to the Cracow University.

Between 1548 and 1556 when Queen Bona was in residence in the Warsaw Castle there were great treasures here. No list of them has been preserved but we can assume that Bona's valuables comprised not only gold ducats but also various works of art made of gold and precious stones. The only one of these items still remaining in Warsaw is a gold goblet which the queen gave to the Collegiate Church of St. John's; the rest went with her on her return to Italy, when she left Poland for ever.

' A magnificent collection of artistic objects was assembled by King Sigismund Augustus, in which pride of place was given to about 350 tapestries, commissioned in Flanders between 1548 and 1567. This collection consisted of four series of figural tapestries showing "The Story of Paradise", "The Story of Noah", also known as "The Flood", "The Story of Moses", and "The Story of the Tower of Babel", as well as other hangings of various sizes on animal and landscape themes and with grotesque motifs, also with the design of the coats-of-arms of Poland and Lithuania and the initials of Sigismund Augustus in them. These hangings were made in the Brussels studios of Willem Pannemaker, Pieter van Aelst, Nicolas Leyniers, and Jan van Tigen, according to cartoons by the Flemish painters Michiel van Cox and Willem Tons.

The tapestries from the collection of Sigismund Augustus are some of the most magnificent works of art ever made on the instigation of a Polish patron. The animal-landscape series is of an exceptional and unique nature and no similar tapestries can be found among any of the other European collections. The figural tapestries, made according to the cartoons of Cox, are certainly not unique works of art as the same Brussels studios executed several other series now found in Germany, Austria, and Spain, but Sigismund Augustus' tapestries surpass them in the quality of workmanship as they were prototypes for the later copies.

These tapestries were commissioned by Sigismund Augustus for the decoration of the rooms in the Wawel Royal Castle in Cracow but at various periods they also adorned other royal residences including the Warsaw Castle. When the king died without an heir the whole collection was left to the Commonwealth. As a result the tapestries became the property of the state and the Royal Grand Treasurer was responsible for looking after and arranging them. Out of the original collection only 136 have been preserved until modern times — five of them are in the Warsaw Royal Castle collection and the others are in the Wawel.

Sigismund Augustus liked to surround himself with beautiful objects and had a particular predilection for collecting jewels. Bernardo Bongiovanni, the apostolic nuncio in Poland, wrote in 1560 that "in his room he has a table from wall to wall on which there are 16 boxes of two span in length and one and a half span in width, filled with jewels... including the Charles V ruby, also the latter's diamond medal of the size of the 'Agnus Dei', which has an eagle on one side, and two pillars on the other with the inscription 'plus ultra'. Apart from these there is a mass of rubies and emeralds, both rough and cut ones... in a word I saw more jewels than I ever expected to see assembled in one place with which the Venetian and papal collections, which I have also seen, cannot be compared".

The jewels, like the tapestries, were left to the state in the king's will. They were kept in the royal treasury in the Wawel until the end of the 18th century when they suffered the rapaciousness of Frederick II of Prussia after the third partition of Poland. Only a few items have been preserved until modern times, which can be identified as objects dating from the former Jagiellonian collection and are scattered among various museums on both hemispheres today. The Metropolitan Museum of Art in New York has a splendid medallion framed in gold and decorated with multi-coloured enamel with the likeness of Queen Bona sculpted on it in chalcedony. This medallion was made by the famous Italian artist Gian Jacopo Caraglio, who worked in Cracow for Sigismund I and Sigismund Augustus. The

Hermitage in Leningrad has a piece by the same artist, a beautiful cameo brooch in sardonyx with a bust of Sigismund Augustus on it, while the cathedral treasury in Uppsala in Sweden has one of Catherine the Jagiellonian's necklaces (she was the wife of John III Vasa, King of Sweden). This necklace is made from gold and coloured enamel, decorated with diamonds and rubies in the shape of the letter "C" (Catherine) beneath a crown, and is one of a set of necklaces which Sigismund I commissioned in Nuremberg in 1546 from the jewellery master Nicolas Nonarth for his daughters Sophia, Anna, and Catherine, with their initials on each one. The National Museum in Warsaw has a pendant in the shape of an eagle made of rock crystal which tradition vaguelly links with the name of Sigismund Augustus.

In his reports, the nuncio Bongiovanni, mentioned above, also enumerated the king's expensive cutlery, the weapons on display, his saddles, etc. "They are made of pure gold and silver, which shouldn't surprise one in the least, but they are also masterpieces of the kind no one would believe who has not seen them." Items which aroused particular admiration in the papal diplomat were the twelve suits of display armour belonging to Sigismund Augustus and especially "one suit with beautiful sculpture and figures made of silver showing all of the victories achieved by the king's ancestors in Muscovy".

One of the suits of armour which Bongiovanni saw was given by Queen Anna the Jagiellonian to her brother-in-law, John III of Sweden, after the death of Sigismund Augustus. It is a magnificent set of armour, both for horse and rider, made in the middle of the 16th century by the excellent Nuremberg armourer Kunz Lochner. Its surface is covered with multi-coloured gilded Renaissance decoration composed of arabesque motifs. Since the 16th century it has been kept in the royal Livrustkammaren in Stockholm. Another suit of armour for a boy, which belonged to Sigismund Augustus, decorated with smooth gilded geometric designs and made in the workshop of Joerg Seusenhofer, the Innsbruck armourer, is now in the National Museum in Budapest.

Rich artistic collections were assembled in the Castle by the next kings of the house of Vasa — Sigimund III,

Ladislaus IV, and John Casimir. We know that Sigismund III was a painter, sculpted in amber, and even made his own jewellery and gold articles. The king's fondness for artistic handicrafts aroused the astonishment and disgust of the gentry who saw a good sovereign as one who was a craftsman in military matters. Sigismund III's weakness for beautiful things was particularly evident in his passion for collecting *objets d'art*, especially paintings by Italian masters. He had special royal agents active in Italy who bought up paintings and collected information about prices and new artistic talents. Some pictures by Antonio Vasilacchi on allegorical subjects were brought from Venice to the Polish court and these show the legend of Diana and Caliosto, and religious paintings like "The Courage of St. Ursula", "The Courage of St. Ladislaus", "The Courage of St. Dimitri", etc. The same painter, in partnership with Palma the Younger, did a series of paintings for Sigismund III on the subject of the legend of Eros and Psyche. We know that Crown Prince Ladislaus on his tour of Western Europe in 1624 visited the studios of Guido Reni and Guercino and other painters. In Mantua the Duke (of the house of Gonzaga) gave his Polish guest "some paintings by famous old masters" and in Brussels the Crown Prince had his portrait painted by Rubens. He also commissioned him to do a portrait of his father Sigismund III.

The Polish court was in touch with Jan Bruegel the Elder and in 1621 the painter wrote about it to Cardinal Federigo Borromeo: "I have sent many paintings to the King of Poland who likes our work". Jan Bruegel the Younger boasted in a letter to the same addressee that the prices for his father's paintings which he had received from the Polish Crown Prince were of the highest and the Crown Prince "has almost all his paintings". We know that in 1637 a Polish emissary bought for Ladislaus IV the paintings "The Infant Jesus and St. John the Baptist in a garland of roses" from the studio of Daniel Seghers, painted in the style of Cornelis Schut. In 1645 Queen Marie Louise acquired from Seghers' studio a picture showing St. Anne in the garland of flowers which was the joint work of Seghers and Erasmus Quellinus the

Younger. After the death of Rubens, when his family was auctioning off his collection, Ladislaus IV was the largest buyer after the court at Madrid..

Works of art were the best kind of present for Sigismund III. He acquired pictures from the legations of the European courts and also from the famous Jesuit, Poss-evino. The custom existed at that time of friendly courts exchanging portraits of members of their families. We know that the Florentine Medicis sent Sigismund III their portraits and received in turn the portraits of the Polish royal family (now in the Uffizi Gallery in Florence). When Ladislaus IV was widowed he received from the Emperor Ferdinand III "a selection of 16 portraits of archduchesses". On the same occasion the French court sent him nine portraits of French princesses to choose from.

Foreign purchases and gifts from foreign courts and legations still did not satisfy the artistic demands of Sigismund III and later of Ladislaus IV. To put into effect the many and varied enterprises a personal court of artists was necessary. At the service of the successive Vasa monarchs was a numerous group of artists of various nationalites among whom first place was occupied by Tommaso Dolabella, an Italian who gradually became completely polonized. He specialized in large canvases on historical and military subjects. The other artists were mainly portrait painters, whose work consisted of numerous portraits of the Polish Vasa kings, their families, and entourage, which have been preserved until today. The largest set of portraits of the Polish royal family which numbers at least twenty is kept in the Bavarian State Collection and formed the dowry of Anna Catherina Constance, the daughter of Sigismund III, who in 1642 married Philip William of Neuburg, later the Palatine Elector. These portraits without doubt originally deco-rated the rooms of various Warsaw royal residences, including the Castle. Several of them have recently been returned to the Castle as a gift from the government of the Federal Republic of Germany for the recreated Castle collection.

Thus it can be seen that the art collections of the Polish Vasas were rich and varied. In spite of the fact that no lists or inventories have been preserved we can assume that there were many items by famous European painters. The French diplomat, Jean le Laboureur, who has already been mentioned several times, noticed that the Castle Chapel "was adorned with many pictures painted by the most famous artists". Unforunately the Vasa gallery suffered destruction and dispersal during the Swedish and Brandenburg invasion of 1655—57. The remains of the gallery which were preserved in Warsaw were taken to France by John Casimir after his abdication. There were only 130 pictures but even among these few there were several names of famous masters like Rembrandt, Rubens, Jordaens, Guido Reni, Guercino, Bruegel, Bassano, etc.

Also two magnificent paintings by Rembrandt, "Portrait of a Rabbi" and "Portrait of a Man with Pearls on his Hat", come from the Vasa collections. These pictures were probably bought by John Casimir but he did not take them with him to France. They remained in Warsaw till 1720 when Augustus II removed them together with other pictures from the Warsaw royal residences to Dresden. Since this time they have been the pride of the famous Dresden Art Gallery. The other portraits of the Vasa gallery which did not suffer destruction were scattered around the world. Today we can point out only a few of them in foreign art galleries which we know to have come from the former Vasa collections, e.g. an equestrian portrait of Sigismund III painted in Rubens' studio is in Gripsholm Castle, and a portrait of Ladislaus IV from the same studio is in the Metropolitan Museum in New York.

Apart from pictures in the Vasa collections there were also many tapestries which decorated the kings' rooms. Sigismund III made full use of the large collection of tapestries of Sigismund Augustus of which some series were used to decorate the Castle rooms. The collection was increased by Sigismund III with the addition of tens of new hangings. He brought 20 Flemish tapestries with him from Sweden which made up the series of "The Story of the Trojan War", "The Story of Absalom", and "The Story of Saul". He inherited two series, "The Story of Octavio August" and "The Story of Julius Caeser" from his father and obtained ten tapestries showing "The Story of Scipio" as a gift from the Elector of Brandenburg. In the royal collection there was also a series of tapestries showing scenes from the Polish-Muscovite War of 1609—10. These were probably made in Poland like the tapestries with the coats-of-arms of Poland, Lithuania, Sweden, and the house of Vasa which were taken to Bavaria as a dowry by Anna Catherine Constance. In 1624 the Polish court commissioned a series of ten tapestries interwoven with gold thread showing "The Tasks of Ulysses" at the studio of the weaver Jakôb Guebels the Younger in Brussels. We know that Ladislaus IV made negotiations for the purchase of seven tapestries with battle scenes, including one which was to show the siege of Smolensk, from the studio of van der Gucht.

When John Casimir left Poland after his abdication he took with him twelve series composed of 88 tapestries. These were the series Sigismund III had previously brought from Sweden consisting of "The Story of the Trojan War", "The Story of Saul", "The Story of Absalom", "The Story of Scipio" and "The Tasks of Ulysses". Some of the later purchases of Ladislaus IV and John Casimir were the series, "The Story of Astraea" and "The History of the Jews" as well as four tapestries with grotesque borders showing "The Labours of Hercules" and "The Triumph of Bacchus". All of these tapestries were interwoven with gold thread. The most modest ones are "The Story of Constantine" and two other series — one composed of seven battle scenes and another made up of eight tapestries with hunting scenes.

In the 16th and 17th centuries various kinds of oriental tapestries and particularly knotted and short-cut Persian rugs were especially popular in Poland. There were many of these also in the Vasa collections. They were purchased by the Polish court through the agency of Armenian merchants who had settled in Lvov. In 1601 Sigismund III commissioned a series of carpets decorated with the Polish eagle and the Vasa Wheatsheaf in Kashan, at that time the most famous centre for carpet weaving in Persia. Five of them, which come from the wedding trousseau of Anna Catherine Constance, have been preserved until today in the state collections in Munich. Oriental carpets were also a traditional gift to the kings of Poland from Turkish and Tartar emissaries and many were derived from the many conquests during the wars between Poland and the Muslim world.

Silver was particularly popular during the Baroque period. Table services, chandeliers, luxurious cutlery, and even various items of furniture, chests, caskets, altar-pieces, etc., were made then as earlier from silver. We know that Ladislaus IV, when he was still Crown Prince, had a bed of ebony inlaid with silver. At the end of the 16th century the Augsburg workshop of Matthias Wallbaum was famous for its production of such altar-pieces and caskets. Many of his products also found their way into the royal collections. A room altar-piece by Wallbaum was given to the Płock cathedral treasury by Queen Constance. Another altar-piece made of ebony and silver and an ornate chest, a gift from Queen Marie-Louise, are kept in the Warsaw Convent of Visitation Sisters. Sigismund III left in his will to Crown Prince John Albert "a silver altar-piece with six large silver candle holders and a silver cross made in Augsburg". Finally let us mention the twelve figures of the Apostles "of pure gold cast on ebony bases" and gold statues of Christ, the Madonna, and St. Sigismund the Martyr which were in the possession of Sigismund III, to illustrate the variety and wealth of the artistic collections of the Polish Vasas.

John III Sobieski assembled a large artistic collection at the Castle, consisting mainly of various West-European and oriental (Persian and Turkish) fabrics. The inventories from this period give lists of the many tapestries, coverings of patterned velvet, silk fabrics, carpets interwoven with gold and silver, and canopies embroidered with gold thread and pearls. The king kept his private treasury in the Castle and we know the contents of it from a detailed list which was made in 1696 straight after the sovereign's death. There were miniatures of foreign monarchs in expensive frames inlaid with precious stones, gold and silver belts, and, first and foremost, display arms which were John III's passion, like daggers with expensive scabbards, sabres with hilts set with precious stones, powder-horns adorned with gold, etc.

This collection was the private property of the Sobieski

family and therefore after the death of the king it passed into the ownership of his heirs, Queen Dowager Marie-Casimire and the royal children James, Alexander, and Constantine.

During the reign of Augustus II and Augustus III of the Saxon house of Wettin there were no major art collections at the Castle. Both of these monarchs had a weakness for fine arts but the collections which they assembled were kept in Dresden, the capital of Saxony of which they were electors. At their instigation the famous Dresden collection was begun, including the splendid Art Gallery where two pictures by Rembrandt, as mentioned above, are found which were taken there from Poland, and also a rich jewel collection, the Gruenes Gewelbe, where many Polish items were kept. In Poland, where the Wettin dynasty did not manage to make the throne hereditary in spite of their efforts, no major artistic collections or cultural institutions came into existence on their initiative. The Castle rooms were furnished with the small number of items necessary to maintain the official nature of the building. Many of the furnishings, like the furniture, pictures, etc,, were the private property of the Wettins and after the death of Augustus III they were taken back to the electoral court in Dresden. A large painting by Johann Samuel Mock showing the grand manoeuvres of the Polish and Saxon forces on the field of Czerniaków in 1732 is a case in point. This picture decorated the Audience Chamber in the Warsaw Castle, and after 1763 it was placed in Dresden. Now the government of the German Democratic Republic has presented this painting to the Castle as a gift.

The artistic patronage of Stanislaus Augustus, the last king of Poland, had a great influence on the development of modern Polish culture and the collection assembled by the king — in spite of the fact that it has been considerably reduced over the years — is still the pride of the Castle collection today. Stanislaus Augustus' great wish was to found an Academy of Fine Arts in Warsaw but he never managed to fulfil this wish. Instead of an academy he established Marcello Bacciarelli's "studio" at the Castle where many artistic talents were trained. Many Polish painters who were active at the end of the 18th century "graduated" from Bacciarelli's studio. For the more than thirty years of his reign Stanislaus Augustus assembled pictures, engravings, and sculptures as academic aids for his future academy. His Plaster Mould Department, in which copies of the most famous ancient and modern sculptures were gathered, had a similar aim. This collection was presented to the University of Warsaw in the 19th century or more exactly to the Faculty of Fine Arts. In autumn 1939 the collection was almost completely destroyed.

The Royal Drawing Department was also established with the Academy of Fine Arts in mind. At the end of the 18th century it contained around 100,000 drawings and etchings, placed in beautiful albums decorated with the royal coat-of-arms. In 1818 the Royal Drawing Department was included in the Warsaw University Library. During the last war 60,000 drawings and etchings vanished, partly as a result of theft and "safety protection" by German "scholars". The items preserved from the former collection are today an inestimable source of knowledge about Polish art during the period of the Enlightenment.

In 1795 the royal book collection amounted to 15,580 volumes. It contained books on various fields of learning including many works devoted to art, often in elegant and rare editions. In 1805 the royal library was purchased by Tadeusz Czacki for the *lycée* in Krzemieniec but after the November Insurrection in 1831 the tsarist authorities removed it to Kiev where it was incorporated in the St. Vladimir University Library as a separate section, known as the *Collectio Regia*.

There was also a rich collection of glyptic art at the Castle, i.e. miniature sculptures in precious stones, and also copies of the most famous cameos and intaglios, a coin collection, models of machines and various scientific instruments, including astronomical ones with which the astronomer-cum-priest Stefan Łuskina observed the heavens from the castle tower. There was also a rich collection of classical sculpture, assembled with great effort and at enormous cost.

However, the most valuable collection was the art gallery which at the end of the reign of Stanislaus Augustus had 2,200 items. The royal collection included many masterpieces by old Italian, Flemish, and Dutch masters. There are now scarcely 200 pictures from the former royal collection in Warsaw collections, the rest having been scattered all over the world. Of the six Rembrandts owned by Stanislaus Augustus only two have remained in Warsaw: the small but dramatic "Self Portrait" and "Portrait of Marten Soolmans". Two others, "The Jewish Bride" and "Portrait of the Bride's Father" were until recently in the Kunsthistorisches Museum in Vienna. "Portrait of the Artist's Brother" is in the Louvre in Paris and the most famous and most beautiful painting by Rembrandt ever in Polish hands, "The Polish Cavalryman", adorns the Frick Collection in New York, sold in 1910 by the owner at that time, Count Zdzisław Tarnowski of Dzików.

For Stanislaus Augustus collecting paintings resulted from a profound understanding of the educational role of art collections and their place in the cultural enlightenment of the community. The king had intended to convert his rich and varied collections into public museums in the future. However, this intention was only partly put into effect and certainly not in a way that the king would have desired. At least the scattered royal collection has remained at the service of culture and learning until the present time in various places at home and abroad. There is no major museum in Poland which does not possess a work of art from Stanislaus Augustus' collection and in many foreign museums they are the highlights of the collections. In the 19th century the Castle collections were not enlarged. During the constitutional Kingdom of Poland which was joined in personal union to Russia, the parliamentary rooms and the royal apartments remained in the same state as during the reign of Stanislaus Augustus. After the collapse of the November Insurrection in 1831 the majority of the historical Castle furnishings, including the pictures based on themes from Polish history, the royal portraits, and the busts of famous Poles, as well as the paintings by Bernardo Bellotto, were all carried away either to Moscow or to St. Petersburg on the orders of Tsar Nicholas I.

After independence had been regained in 1918 a new

chapter in the history of the Castle collection began. All historical paintings, sculptures, furniture, etc., were returned from Soviet Russia between 1922 and 1924 which allowed the Castle rooms to be restored to their appearance under Stanislaus Augustus. In 1922 the Department of the National Art Collections was created at the Castle which had as its task to look after works of art in historical residences which belonged to the head of state. With the small funds available to it the Department purchased a series of works of art which were of particular importance for Polish culture and history. Jan Matejko's "Rejtan" was bought from the collection of the former imperial museum in Vienna and "Báthory at Pskov" by the same painter was purchased from Count Benedykt Tyszkiewicz. A magnificent 16th century silk Persian rug of the Kashan type was acquired from the Wilanów collection; this was one of the finest examples of this kind of carpet in Europe and was also distinguished by its exceptional size (760 by 350 cm). A portrait of Stefan Czarniecki painted by Brodero Matthisen was bought from the former Berlin imperial castle in 1926 as were two splendid tapestries made in the second half of the 16th century, probably in Poland, taken from the series "The Story of Samson" and woven with the coat-of-arms of Dymitri Chalecki, and also other works of art. An urn with the heart of Tadeusz Kościuszko was placed in the Royal Chapel in 1927 after having been brought from the Polish Museum in Rapperswil in Switzerland.

The Castle collections were also enriched by an exceptionally large and valuable collection of tapestries, pictures, period furniture, bronze and porcelain brought to the Castle by Stanisław Krosnowski. Valuable gifts were presented also by the Szlubowski family, Jakub Potocki of Helenów and Adam Branicki of Wilanów whose donations included an illuminated manuscript of the Florentine school from the end of the 15th century used as a prayer-book by Queen Bona. One of the most important donations from an artistic point of view was the large tapestry from the series "The Story of Scipio Africanus" showing "Scipio's Triumphal Procession to the Temple of Jupiter in the Capitol", which was woven in Brussels in 1660 at the studio of Geraert van der Strecken according to the design of Giulio Romano and which was donated in 1934 by Baroness Maria Taube, née Kronenberg.

After the outbreak of war in 1939, in the face of the imminent German invasion some objects of special historical and artistic value were evacuated together with the civil chancellery of the President of the Republic. Thus the two historical pictures by Matejko, the Wilanów carpet, the tapestries with the coat-of-arms of Chalecki, and the royal insignia of Stanislaus Augustus were saved. The royal insignia were placed with the national treasures which were taken from Cracow and transported to Canada where fortunately they survived the war and were eventually returned to Poland. The Matejko paintings were found in Germany in 1945. However, the Chalecki tapestries and the Wilanów carpet vanished.

The present collections of the Royal Castle in Warsaw are composed of the items saved from the original furnishings of the Stanislaus Augustus rooms, the remains of the collections of Stanislaus Augustus, the collection assembled between 1920 and 1939 by the department of the National Art Collections, and those items suitable for their artistic value and character to be placed in the Castle rooms which were presented by the Warsaw National Museum.

A separate section has been created by the numerous gifts presented to the Castle by Poles at home and abroad, various civic organizations, and also by governments and states. It does not often happen in history that one state presents works of art, in many cases of immeasurable historical and artistic value, to another country as an expression of good will. In Poland, where the cultural resources were so terribly devastated in the course of such a barbarous war and occupation, these gifts have a particular importance.

The first official gift to enrich the Castle collections was a series of four portraits — of Anna the Jagiellonian, Stephen Báthory, Prince Sigismund Ladislaus, and Queen Marie-Casimire — presented by the then Foreign Minister of the Federal Republic of Germany, Walter Scheel, during his visit to Warsaw in 1973. The first three portraits were painted by so far unidentified artists, who were active at the Polish court at the end of the 16th century, and they went to Bavaria as part of the dowry of the above-mentioned Princess Anna Catherine Constance. These portraits have a particular value as they probably once decorated the Castle rooms to which they have been restored after over 300 years. The fourth portrait — of Queen Marie-Casimire — also passed into the Bavarian collection through the dowry of another Polish princess, Theresa Cunegund Sobieska, who married Elector Maximilian II of Bavaria in 1695.

In 1973 during the visit of the First Secretary of the Central Committee of the Polish United Workers' Party, Edward Gierek, to Paris, the French company Berliet presented him with a valuable clock in a frame made of gilded bronze and green-coloured horn. This clock was made in 1749 by the French court clock-maker Causard who 'had a charter to sell pendulum clocks in all the provinces where the king travelled. The frame of the clock is the work of the Paris master B. Lieutaud. A similar clock with a frame of gilded bronze and green-coloured horn was once in one of the Castle rooms and described in the 1769 inventory as being of "Parisian workmanship". Perhaps this was a clock made by the same Parisian masters?

An item of exceptional historical value is a painting showing the wedding procession of Sigismund III and Archduchess Constance in 1605, presented in the name of the Swedish government by the then prime minister, Olof Palme, during his visit to Poland in 1974. This water colour and tempera painting on woven paper is of the nature of a frieze with a length of 16.09 m and a width of 0.27 m. Various detachments of the Polish cavalry and infantry are shown on it including a regiment of Hussars with wings made from eagles' feathers attached to their saddles, the Royal Standard-Bearer with the standard of the Kingdom of Poland, Polish and Lithuanian dignitaries, the Primate, the Apostolic nuncio, the ambassadors of other countries, and finally the royal carriages. The authorship of this work has not yet been established. It has been suggested that it was most probably painted by a guild of Cracow artists jointly. It should be added that until the middle of the 17th century the painting was kept in the Warsaw Castle and was taken from there in the course of the frequent wars between Poland and Sweden as a war trophy by King Charles Gustavus and remained in the royal collection of the Livrustkammaren in Stockholm until not long ago. It has now been returned to its original historical place in the Warsaw Castle.

In 1974 Princess Alexandra, on behalf of the British people, presented a splendid set of tapestry-covered furniture from the first half of the 18th century, and the President of the Republic of Austria, Dr. Rudolf Kirchschlaeger, gave a valuable crystal chandelier which came from the Schoenbrunn palace collection. In 1975 during his visit to Poland, Valery Giscard d'Estaing, the President of the French Republic, presented a silver vase, the work of the 18th century Warsaw goldsmith, Jan Jerzy Bandau, and a beautiful desk made by the excellent French cabinet-maker, David Roentgen.

One gift of unusual artistic and historical value which has recently enriched the Castle collection is a set of various historical memorabilia and works of art, handed over to Edward Gierek by the Government of the Soviet Union in 1977. Among the items are standards from the Kościuszko Insurrection of 1794 and the national uprisings of 1831 and 1863. Of particular interest is the standard from the November Insurrection with an inscription in Polish and Russian — "In the name of God, for our freedom and yours". Also of value are four Polish swords, three with the initials of Stanislaus Augustus on them and the fourth with the inscription "The people with the King, the King with the People", dated 3 May 1791. This kind of inscription was often engraved on sword hilts by the advocates of the Third of May Constitution. Also among these gifts is a set of paintings by Polish artists of the 19th century, mainly pupils of the Academy of Fine Arts in St. Petersburg. The most valuable item however is a magnificent Flemish tapestry shot through with gold thread showing "The Seizure of Mortal Women by the Sons of the Gods" which dates from the second half of the 16th century. This tapestry was once part of the collection of Sigismund

Augustus. Now it is the pride of the Castle rooms, recalling the magnificent beneficence of this sovereign.

Of great value to the Castle collections are four royal portraits donated by Chancellor Helmut Schmidt on behalf of the government of the Federal Republic of Germany in 1977. They are full-length likenesses of Sigismund the Old, Queen Bona, their daughter Isabella the Jagiellonian, Queen of Hungary, and a portrait of Sigismund III. These portraits passed into German possession through marriages. The first three were probably taken with her by Sophia, the daughter of Sigismund I and Bona, when she married Henry II, Duke of Brunswick in 1556, and the fourth comes from the marriage dowry of Anna Catherine Constance. There were formerly only a few portraits of the Jagiellonian dynasty in Polish collections and these three magnificent likenesses of Sigismund I, Bona, and Isabella have been a valuable contribution and have also put more light on early Polish portrait painting.

A valuable gift which has formed the furnishings for one of the Castle rooms is a set of furniture, porcelain, pictures, etc., which was donated by the government of the German Democratic Republic. Of particular interest are the portraits of Augustus III, King of Poland and Elector of Saxony, and his family, and a large painting by Mock showing the review of the Polish and Saxon troops at Czerniaków. As we have already mentioned this picture hung in the Castle Audience Chamber in the first half of the 18th century and after the death of Augustus III, as it was the private property of the Wettin family, it was taken to Dresden. The reacquisition of this historically valuable painting which was once part of the furnishings of the royal apartments is of particular importance for the Castle collections.

Equally valuable are the gifts to the Castle by various private individuals and organizations. At the time of going to press the Book of Gifts drawn up by the Committee for the Rebuilding of the Royal Castle had 1,566 items listed. The list begins with a beautiful portrait of Jan Andrzej Morsztyn, ascribed to Hyacinthe Rigaud and originating from the family collection of the famous poet Ludwik Hieronim Morstin and donated by him to the

Castle in 1966. A series of historical items was presented by the Marquis Eugène Kucharski, resident in France, including portraits of Queen Marie Leszczyńska (wife of Louis XV) by Jean Marc Nattier and the Dauphin and Madame Royale, the children of Louis XVI, painted by the Polish artist, Alexandre Kucharski who had settled in France. Professor Bolesław Gawecki donated two portraits dating from 1775 and showing Antonio Crutto, an oriental languages interpreter of Albanian origin who was active at the court of Stanislaus Augustus, and his wife. It should be emphasized here that these portraits were the only articles which Professor Gawecki managed to take with him from burning Warsaw in September 1944. The gift of Professor Tomasz Kluz is the painting "The Madonna with a Gold-finch" by Jacopo da Pontormo, which is a copy of the original which is kept in the Hermitage in Leningrad. Many works of art — pictures, clocks, porcelain, and miniatures — were presented by Dr. Wanda Majewska of Jedlnia near Radom, and Dr. Juliusz Godlewski of Switzerland donated a travelling chest decorated with the coat-of-arms of the Mniszech family.

The Kalkstein family gave two marble medallions from the 18th century with likenesses of Augustus III and Stanislaus Augustus, Mrs. Stefania Raczkowska née Stecka of Zakopane donated a Baroque chest of drawers with the Polish and Saxon coats-of-arms on it, Colonel Roman Umiastowski of London presented two large globes of the Heavens and the Earth which were made by Coronelli, a geographer active in Venice in the 17th century, and Mrs. Maria Steckiewicz donated a silver turret-style clock, signed "Jacob Stevensen 1600", on behalf of the Kijakowski family (according to the family tradition of the donor, one of her ancestors had received this clock from King Stanislaus Augustus). Mr. Henryk Koterba who lives near Warsaw, a gilder by profession who makes artistic frames for pictures, and his son, Edward, who lives in Hollywood, presented the Castle with valuable pictures, sculptures, and porcelain, including a preliminary sketch by Bacciarelli for the coronation portrait of Stanislaus Augustus, and Professor Edmund Zawacki of the University of Wisconsin at

Madison gave a set of Biedermeier furniture. The owner of a famous Warsaw firm of reproduction light fittings, Mr. Piotr Mielczarek, donated a reproduction crystal chandelier which decorates the Canaletto Room. A beautiful clock from the beginning of the 19th century was the gift of Mrs. Henryka Walińska of New York, and Mrs. Teresa Sahakian who lives in Belgium donated a series of valuable items including six tapestries with birds of paradise and floral motifs, made in the first half of the 18th century at Aubusson. A set of various historical objects, amounting to 270 items in all — furniture, paintings, bronze work, clocks, and porcelain, including a collection of Polish and Silesian glassware — come from the will of the famous collector and antique dealer, Tadeusz Wierzejski.

One of the last works by Jan Matejko which until recently was in private ownership was a small painting (73 by 66 cm) entitled "The Poisoning of Duke Janusz" (the last of the Mazovian Dukes). This painting was donated in 1977 by its last owner, Mrs. Florentyna Rotter. It should be mentioned here that this painting was rolled up in a rucksack by its owners and taken from Warsaw during the 1944 Uprising.

Representatives of the Bydgoszcz voivodship donated five portraits of Polish kings — Boleslaus the Brave, Boleslaus the Wry-mouth, Mieszko II, Wenceslas of Bohemia, and Casimir the Jagiellonian — painted at the end of the 18th century by Jan Bogumił Plersch. A really royal offering was made by the Friends of Warsaw Society who bought a Brussels tapestry from around 1560 showing David and Abigail, originating from the former Tarnowski collection, with money collected from members of the Society. The Austrian firm of Vöest-Alpine and the Polish company Polimex-Cekop of Warsaw bought portraits of Stefan Czarniecki and one of the sons of Augustus III who was Crown Prince of Poland. The Warsaw Association of Private Shopkeepers acquired for the Castle with their own money a splendid Empire clock made of gilded bronze of French workmanship. The manager of the Northern Natural Gas Company of the US, Willis A. Strauss, donated a valuable portrait of Prince Joseph Poniatowski painted by Grassi.

At the instigation of the Paris Committee for the Rebuilding of the Castle a presentation was made of over 300 books with artistic bindings from the 18th century to the future Royal Library. The same aim was served by many gifts in the form of books, albums, drawings, documents, and letters, many of which have flowed into the Castle in recent years. The writer Stanisław Szenic donated a book with an artistic binding with the book-plate of Stanislaus Augustus originating from the former Royal Library, and Dr. Bronisław Kristall presented a splendid album with drawings illustrating festivities at the French court, entitled *Festiva ad Capita Annulumque de Cursio a Rege Lodovico XIV...* published in Paris in 1670. This album has the ex libris of Louis XIV imprinted on the binding and once belonged to his library at Versailles. Of great historical value is a drawing with a diagram and inventory of the ruins of the Emperor Hadrian's villa at Tivoli, made in 1781 with the dedication "To His Majesty Stanislaus Augustus, King of Poland, the Patron of the arts, from Francesco Piranesi, architect, with the most humble respect". This drawing was donated by Count Emeryk Hutten Czapski who was resident in Rome. Of the many valuable items let us also mention Bartosz Paprocki's *Nest of Virtue,* the baronage published in Cracow in 1578, given by Mr. Antoni Marszewski of Warsaw, and the letters of Stanislaus Augustus and Tadeusz Kościuszko, given by Mrs. Janina Gąbska of Łódź.

The gifts donated to the Castle by the official representatives of foreign states are an expression of the recognition of Poland's general respect for tradition and cultural treasures and of the hard task undertaken in the rebuilding of the historical monuments destroyed in the war. For the Poles there is also an additional reason for pleasure. These gifts housed in the rooms of the Royal Castle in Warsaw, by enriching the historical collections saved from the holocaust of the last war, will always bear witness to the good will of other nations towards Poland and the common source and unity of European culture.

However, how are we to evaluate the gifts from private individuals, from the many Poles living at home and abroad, people of various walks of life, sometimes very wealthy but more often only of modest means? Apart

from their artistic and historical worth, the items presented by them always have a considerable financial value and
are often the only family mementoes or articles of value
saved from the destruction of wars, articles which in more
than one case could ensure the owner prosperity or even
wealth. These people have freely given up such desires
in the name of their ties with their country and its culture.

ILLUSTRATIONS

View of Warsaw at the end of the 16th century. Drawing from *Theatri praecipurum totius mundi liber sextus* by G. Braun and F. Hogenberg, published in 1618

Portrait of Conrad III the Red-haired, Duke of Mazovia, by an unknown artist (16th cent.)

Group portrait of Dukes Janusz III and Stanislaus I of Mazovia and their sister, Anna, by an unknown artist (probably 16th cent.)

Portraits of Queen Bona and Sigismund I, by unknown artists (16th cent) gifts
of the German Federal government

Portrait of King Sigismund I the Old, possibly after Hans Duerer

Portrait of Zofia Tarnowska née Odrowąż, wife of Castellan and daughter of
Anna of Mazovia, by an unknown artist (16th cent.)

Portrait of Queen Barbara Radziwiłł, by an unknown artist (an 18th cent.
copy of an earlier painting)

Portrait of King Stephen Báthory, by an unknown artist (16th cent.), donated by the German Federal government

The Polish Seym with King Casimir the Jagiellonian

Portrait of Castellan Jan Krzysztof Tarnowski, husband of Zofia Odrowąż, by an unknown artist (16th cent.)

Portrait of Queen Anna the Jagiellonian, by an unknown artist (16th cent.)

Portrait of Jadwiga Mniszech, mother of the Empress Marina,
by an unknown artist (16th cent.)

Gothic elevation of the Large House, as it was before 1939

Gothic chamber in the Large House, as it was in 1970

Statuta

Regni Poloniae, in ordinem Alphabeti digesta.

A Joanne Herborto, Castellano Lubaczouiensi, Succamerario Premisliensi, et Sacrae Maiestatis Regiae Secretario.

Cum Gratia et Priuilegio Regiae Maiestatis, Lazarus Andreae excudebat Crac. Anno Do-
M. D. LXIII.

Hetman Stanisław Żółkiewski presents the captured Tsar Vasili Shuiski to the Seym in 1611. Engraving by Tomasz Makowski after the painting by Tomasso Dolabella

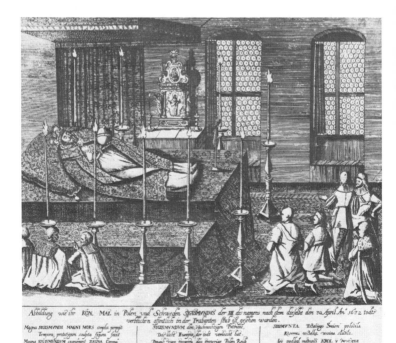

Abbildung wie vir KÖN. MAI. in Polen und Schweden SIGISMVNDVS der III des namens nach dem daselbe den 20 April An 1632 todtr
verstorben offentlich in der Trabanten stub ist gesehen worden.

Magna SIGISMVNDI MAGNI MORS ampla peregit   SIGISMVNDVM den Hochmächtigen Potentat   SIGISMVNTA Tebeligo Smien polonia
Tempora, prototypon sculpta figura facit   Das lutst Europäe, der todt verleschet hat   Ktermu niBeliga weaina dilista.
Magna SIGISMVNDVM exprimunt REGNA, Coronæ   Dem Organ vernommen das fürwürige Polen Reich   Iej padogi mehnuls KROL y Swyciepza
Hæc caput exornas Mors luculenta tuum.   Mit solchen blickett bei dieser Billiun Leich   Tak niema Radej wswywnist Stjina.
                                                  Ph. Jansz fecit Gedo.

The Polish Seym with King Sigismund III. Copperplate engraving by Giacomo Lauri (1622)

Sigismund III laying in state in the Royal Castle in Warsaw. Engraving by F. Jansz (1632)

Portrait of Stanisław Lubomirski, Voivode of Cracow, by an unknown artist
(early 17th cent.)

Portrait of Stanisław Krasiński, Castellan of Płock, by Daniel Schultz

Portrait of Ladislaus IV, by an unknown artist

Portrait of Queen Marie Louise Gonzaga, by Justus van Egmont

Picture illustrating the capitulation of Shein before Ladislaus IV in 1634, by an unknown artist

Portrait of Stefan Czarniecki, Voivode of Ruthenia and Field Hetman of the Crown, by Brodero Matthisen (1659)

Portrait of Stanisław Antoni Szczuka, Speaker of the Seym in 1699 and Chancellor of the Grand Duchy of Lithuania, by an unknown artist

Portrait of Queen Eleonora, daughter of the Emperor Ferdinand III and wife of King Michael Korybut Wiśniowiecki, by an unknown artist

Senate assembly on the electoral field in 1669, etching by an unknown artist

The election of Michael Korybut Wiśniowiecki at Wola near Warsaw in 1669,
etching by an unknown artist

The coronation of Queen Eleonora in St. John's Church in Warsaw in 1670,
etching by an unknown artist

IOANNES III. D. G. REX POLONIARVM, MAGN DVX LITHVAN RVS. PRVS. MA SS
EXERCITVVM CHRISTIANORVM AD VIENNAM CONTRA TVRCAM ET TARTAROS DVCTOR
AC TRIVMPHATOR GLORIOSISSIMVS

King John III Sobieski as victor in the Battle of Vienna of 1683 against
the Turks, drawing by Charles de la Haye after the painting by Jerzy Eleuter
Siemiginowski

Portrait of Franciszek Bieliński, Grand Marshal of Poland 1742—66, by an unknown artist

Portrait of Stanisław Lubomirski, Grand Marshal of Poland 1766—83, by an unknown artist

Bernardo Bellotto-Canaletto: *The Election of Stanislaus Augustus Poniatowski in 1764* (detail)

Marcello Bacciarelli: coronation portrait of Stanislaus Augustus

Mateusz Tokarski: portrait of the Primate Michał Poniatowski with a plan of Jabłonna palace

Mateusz Tokarski: portrait of Adam Naruszewicz, poet and historian, from the book *History of the Polish Nation*

Kazimierz Wojniakowski: *Swearing an Oath to the Constitution on 3 May 1791 in the Senatorial Chamber in the Castle*

Johann Samuel Mock: *The Entry of Augustus III into Warsaw after His Coronation in 1734*

Franciszek Paderewski: portrait of Prince Joseph Poniatowski

Marcello Bacciarelli: *The Granting of the Constitution to the Duchy of Warsaw by Napoleon*

The Opening of the First Seym of the Duchy of Warsaw in 1818; coloured lithograph

View of the Castle in the first half of the 19th century, by an unknown artist

Demonstration on 15 August 1831 in Castle Square during the November
Insurrection; lithograph after the drawing by Feliks Piwarski

Patriotic demonstration in Castle Square in 1861; woodcut from the *Illustrations*
magazine

Jan Matejko: *Rejtan* (detail)

Vaulted room from the reign of Sigismund III, as it was before 1939

The Early Baroque Grodzka (Town) Gate, as it was before 1939

Cartouche with the coat-of-arms of the Commonwealth: part of the rococo
decoration on the Castle façade on the Vistula side, as it was before 1939

Rococo cartouche with the initials of King Augustus III: part of the decoration on the Castle façade on the Vistula side, as it was before 1939

194

Allegorical representation of Lithuania; one of the statues on the parapet of the Castle wing on the Vistula side, as it was before 1939

The Assembly Hall, as it was before 1939

The Knights' Hall, as it was before 1939

The Throne Room, view of the royal throne, as it was before 1939

The Audience Chamber, as it was before 1939

Marcello Bacciarelli: *The Union of Lublin*, one of the historical
paintings in the Knights' Hall

A piece of the rotating clock which disappeared during the war and according
to tradition was presented to the king by Pope Pius VI

The Throne Room, view of the entrance to the Conference Room, as it was
before 1939

The Conference Room, with portraits of the European sovereigns who were ruling contemporary with Stanislaus Augustus, as it was before 1939

Marcello Bacciarelli: an allegorical representation of Strength, an overdoor from the Audience Chamber

A porcelain table top with a miniature showing the story of Telemachus and the nymph Calypso; made in Sèvres in 1777

An original wall painting by Jan Bogumił Plersch in the Conference Room, as seen today

Faience vase from the royal pottery works in the Belvedere, end of the 18th cent.

An original Hercules mask placed on the fireplace in the Audience Chamber,
as seen today

The burning Sigismund Tower on 17 September 1939

Extinguishing the fire in the Ball Room on 17 September 1939

The King's Bedroom after "Black Sunday", 17 September 1939

View of the Sigismund Tower from Świętojańska Street, as seen during the
Warsaw Uprising of August-September 1944

Newspaper headlines about the decision to rebuild the Royal Castle

The Castle ruins, as seen in 1945

The ceremony of starting the clock on the Sigismund Tower, 19 July 1974

The south-east corner of the Castle with the Grodzka Tower, as seen today

Placing the cupola on the Sigismund Tower, 6 July 1974

The Ladislaus Tower in the Grand Courtyard, photograph taken in 1978

The Senatorial Gate, as seen today

The dome of the Royal Chapel, as seen today

Work on the reconstruction of the dome in the Royal Chapel

The former Chamber of Deputies, as seen today

The golden pendant in the form of an eagle decorated with pearls and precious stones; according to tradition it once belonged to Sigismund Augustus, from the middle of the 16th century

The signet ring of King Stephen Báthory; the arms of the Commonwealth under a crown and the wolf's teeth arms of the Báthory family with the king's initials- "St. R. P." (Stephanus Rex Poloniae), cut in sapphires; Polish workmanship from 1576—86

The border of a tablecloth which once belonged to Anna the Jagiellonian with the Polish Eagle and the Queen's initials; cross-stitch embroidery; Polish workmanship from the last quarter of the 16th cent.

217

Adolf Boy (?): Portrait of Ladislaus IV in coronation robes

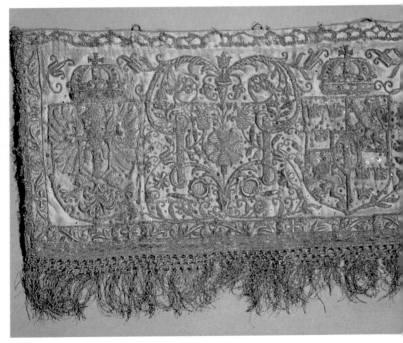

The crown of Ladislaus IV, a detail of the king's portrait

A piece of the garments of Ladislaus IV with an embroidered Polish Eagle and the arms of Sweden; embroidered in gold, silver, and silk; Polish workmanship from the first half of the 17th cent.

Glass goblet with the arms of the Commonwealth, the Janina arms of the Sobieski and the arms of Gdańsk; given to King John III in 1677 by the Gdańsk city council

Coronation robe of King Augustus III; gold and silver embroidery on velvet

Louis de Silvestre: portrait of King Augustus III in Polish costume

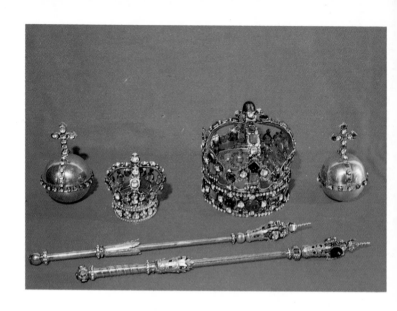

Coronation insignia of Augustus III and Queen Maria Josepha; Dresden
workmanship, 1734

Ceremonial sword of Stanislaus Augustus, made for the coronation of the
king in 1764; Polish workmanship

Flemish tapestry after the drawing by Michiel van Cox, from around the
middle of the 16th century, donated by the USSR government

Portrait of Sigismund III, by an unknown artist, from the end of the 16th cent.,
donated by the German Federal government

Silver clock, the work of the Dutch clockmaker, Jacob Stevensen, from the end of the 16th century, donated by Maria Steckiewicz and the Kijakowski family

French-made mantle clock from the early 18th cent., gift of the Berliet company

The Madonna with a Gold-finch after Jacopo Carrucci, called Pontormo, first half of the 16th cen., donated by Professor Tomasz Kluz

Portrait of Jan Andrzej Morsztyn, ascribed to Hyacinthe Rigaud,
from the late 17th cent., donated by Ludwik Hieronim Morstin

The Flight into Egypt, by an unknown Netherlandish artists of the 16th cent.,
bequeathed by Tadeusz Wierzejski

Detail of the painting showing the wedding procession of Sigismund III and Archduchess Constance in 1606, by an unknown artist, donated by the Swedish government

A tapestry with birds of paradise (detail); one of a series of six tapestries produced by the Aubusson factory in the first half of the 18th cent., donated by Teresa Sahakian

Portrait of Anna Tworkowska, née Radziwiłł, by an unknown artist of the late 17th cent., donated by Ewelina Małachowska-Łempicka

Portrait of Wacław Rzewuski, Grand Hetman of Poland, in the dress of the Order of the White Eagle, by an unknown Polish artist of the second half of the 18th century, donated by Wanda Żeligowska, née Rzewuska

Glass with the monogram of Stanislaus Augustus, from the end of the 18th century, donated by Maria Tabeau and Mieczysław Kasprzyk

Faience plate from the service made in the Belvedere factory in 1776—77 for Sultan Abdul-Hamid I, bequeathed by Tadeusz Wierzejski

Portrait of Prince Xavier, son of Augustus III, by an unknown artist, donated
by the Vöest-Alpine company

Bureau à cylindre in Louis XV-style, a portrait of Queen Marie Leszczyńska of France by Jean Marc Nattier, and a portrait of the Dauphin and Madame Royale by Alexandre Kucharski, donated by the Marquis Eugène Kucharski

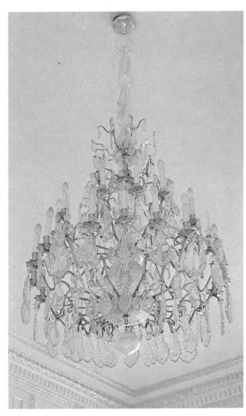

Chandelier of crystal and gilded bronze, intended for the Canaletto Room, donated by Piotr Mielczarek

Marcello Bacciarelli (?): preliminary sketch for the coronation portrait of
Stanislaus Augustus, donated by Henryk Koterba

Turkish cavalrymen, a drawing from *Festiva ad Capita Annulumque de Cursio a Rege Lodovico XIV*, published in Paris in 1670, donated by Dr. Bronisław Kristall

Francesco Piranesi: drawing of Hadrian's villa at Tivoli; detail with the artist's dedication to Stanislaus Augustus, donated by Emeryk Hutten Czapski

Standard from the 1863 Insurrection, donated by the USSR government

Commemorative standard made in 1869 on the 500th anniversary of the death of Casimir the Great, donated by the USSR government

A Polish green and amaranth belt worn with national costume by supporters
of the Third of May Constitution; Polish workmanship of the end of the 18th
century

Jan Matejko: *The Poisoning of Duke Janusz of Mazovia*, donated by Józef and Florentyna Rotter

DIAGRAMS

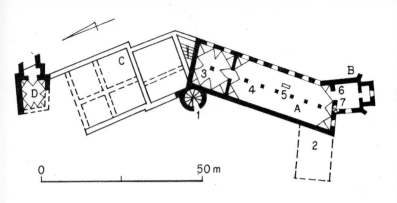

Diagram I. The ground floor of the Castle after the rebuilding under Sigismund Augustus between 1569 and 1572; A — the Large House; B — the Large Tower (Grodzka Tower); C — the new Royal House; D — part of the medieval building; 1 — the Round Tower (entrance to the royal apartments); 2 — building on the south side; 3 — the so-called "One-Pillar Room" (Seym Chancellery); 4 — Chamber of Deputies; 5 — Speaker's Chair (*locus directoralis*); 6 — room in the Large Tower; 7 — stairs leading to the Senatorial Chamber on the first floor (the broken lines signify the probable course of interior walls).
Design by J. Lileyko, drawing by W. Olszowicz.

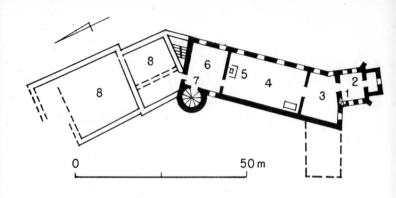

Diagram II. The upper floor of the Castle after the rebuilding under Sigismund Augustus between 1569 and 1572: 1 — stairs leading from the Chamber of Deputies; 2 — room in the Large Tower; 3 — Senatorial Vestibule; 4 — Senatorial Chamber; 5 — royal throne; 6 — the Large Hall; 7 — stairs in the Round Tower; 8 — royal apartments (the broken lines signify the probable course of interior walls). Design by J. Lileyko, drawing by W. Olszowicz.

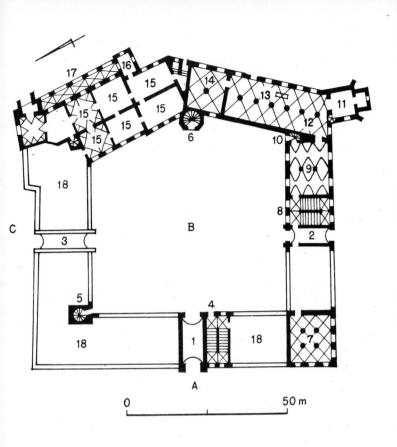

Diagram III. The ground floor of the Castle after the rebuilding under Sigismund III between 1598 and 1619: A — the Front Courtyard; B — the Grand Courtyard; C — the Kitchen Courtyard; 1 — Sigismund Tower Gate; 2 — Grodzka Gate; 3 — a gate later known as the Senatorial Gate; 4 — stairs later known as the Deputies' Staircase; 5 — stairs leading to the royal children's rooms; 6 — the Ladislaus Tower and the stairs leading to the royal apartments; 7 — City of Warsaw Chancellery; 8 — Grand Staircase and the entrance to the parliamentary rooms; 9 — Entrance Hall to the Chamber of Deputies; 10 — stairs to the Senatorial Vestibule; 11 — room in the Grodzka Tower; 12 — Chamber of Deputies; 13 — Speaker's Chair; 14 — Seym Chancellery; 15 — royal apartments; 16 — the so-called Garden Tower; 17 — the arcade gallery; 18 — parts of the Castle without room divisions. Design by J. Lileyko, drawing by W. Olszowicz.

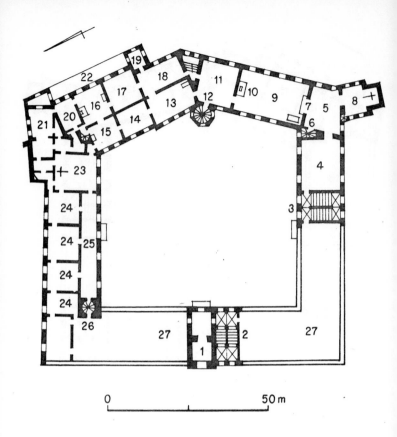

Diagram IV. The upper floor of the Castle after the rebuilding under Sigismund III between 1598 and 1619: 1 — the Sigismund or Royal Tower; 2 — stairs later known as the Deputies' Staircase; 3 — Grand Staircase, leading from the Chamber of Deputies to the Senatorial Chamber; 4 — Entrance Hall to the Senatorial Chamber; 5 — Senatorial Vestibule; 6 — stairs leading from the Entrance Hall to the Chamber of Deputies, also leading to the Theatre Hall on the second floor; 7 — doors leading to the Senatorial Chamber and the Royal Chair; 8 — the Chapel in the Grodzka Tower; 9 — Senatorial Chamber; 10 — royal throne; 11 — Grand Entrance Hall (the Swiss Hall); 12 — stairs in the Ladislaus Tower; 13 — First Ante-room; 14 — Second Ante-room; 15 — Marble Room; 16 — Audience Chamber; 17 — King's Bedroom; 18 — Guards' Room; 19 — study in the Garden Tower; 20 — Queen's Study; 21 — Queen's Bedroom; 22 — terrace; 23 — Chapel; 24 — royal children's rooms; 25 — gallery; 26 — stairs; 27 — parts of the Castle without room divisions.

Design by J. Lileyko, drawing by W. Olszowicz.

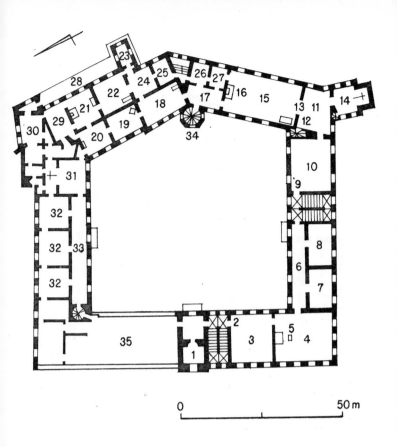

Diagram V. The upper floor of the Castle during the reign of John III (after 1681);
1 — Sigismund Tower; 2 — Deputies' Staircase; 3 — Entrance Hall to the Chamber
of Deputies; 4 — Chamber of Deputies; 5 — Speaker's Chair; 6 — gallery; 7—8 —
chancellery rooms; 9 — Grand Staircase; 10 — Entrance Hall to the Senatorial Chamber; 11 —. Senatorial Vestibule; 12 — stairs leading to the Theatre Hall on the
second floor; 13 — doors leading to the Senatorial Chamber; 14 — Chapel; 15 —
Senatorial Chamber; 16 — royal throne; 17 — entrance hall; 18 — First Ante-room;
19 — Second Ante-room; 20 — Marble Room; 21 — Audience Chamber; 22 —
King's Bedroom; 23 — Bathhouse; 24—27 John III's studies; 28 terrace; 29 —
Queen's Study; 30 — Queen's Bedroom; 31 — Chapel; 32 — Prince Jakub Sobieski's rooms; 33 — gallery; 34 — Ladislaus Tower — stairs to the royal apartments;
35 — parts of the Castle without room divisions.
Design by J. Lileyko, drawing by W. Olszowicz.

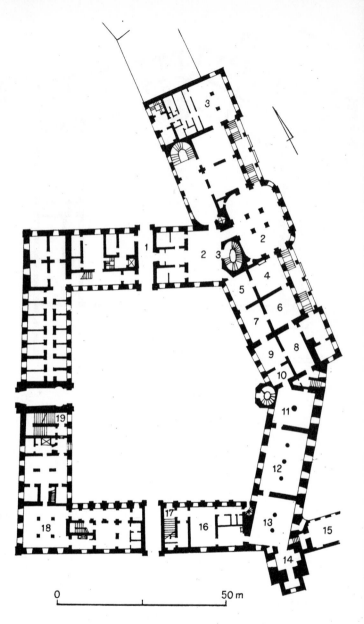

Diagram VI. The ground floor of the Castle after the rebuilding between 1737 and 1746 and after the alterations in the interior design during the reign of Stanislaus Augustus. The Castle as seen today: 1 — Senatorial Gate (entrance for visitors); 2 — Entrance Hall (the way to the cloakroom); 3 — café; 4—10 — the so-called "Jagiellonian Rooms"; 11 — the former Seym Chancellery (the One-Pillar Room); 12—13— the former Chamber of Deputies; 14 — room in the Grodzka Tower; 15 — Royal Library; 16 — former Entrance Hall to the Chamber of Deputies; 17 — Grand Staircase: 18 — former City of Warsaw Chancellery; 19 — Deputies' Staircase.

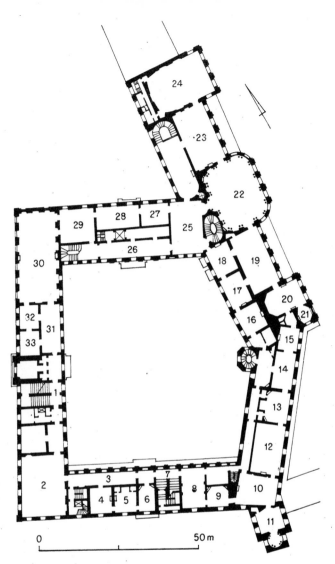

Diagram VII. The upper floor of the Castle after the rebuilding between 1737 and 1746 and after the alterations in the interior design during the reign of Stanislaus Augustus. The Castle as seen today: 1 — Deputies' Staircase; 2 — Chamber of Deputies; 3—6 — chancellery rooms; 7 — Grand Staircase; 8 Guards' Room (the so-called Mier Hall); 9 — Officers' Room; 10 — Room of Views, known as the Canaletto Room; 11 — Chapel; 12 — Audience Chamber; 13 — King's Bedroom; 14—15 — King's Study and Dressing Room; 16 — Green Room; 17 — Yellow Room; 18 — Marble Room; 19 — Knights' Hall; 20 — Throne Room; 21 — Conference Room; 22 — Ball Room; 23 — Council Chamber; 24 — Concert Room (the former Saxon Chapel); 25 — the former ante-room to the Ball Room; 26 — gallery; 27—29 — the former royal children's rooms; 30 — Senatorial Chamber; 31 — the Marshal's Guards' Room; 32 —33 — chancellery rooms.

Graphic layout by Stefan Nargiełło
Production editor: Wiesław Pyszka

This is the one thousand nine hundred and thirty-fifth
publication of Interpress

This book appears also in French and German

Photographs by Z. Jaworski, A. Kotecki, J. Morek, J. Myszkowski, C. Olszewski,
H. Poddębski, J. Rosikoń, and S. Stępniewski; also from the collections of Interpress
Archives, Central Photographic Agency, Art Institute of the Polish Academy
of Sciences, National Museum in Warsaw and Historical Museum of the City
of Warsaw

PRINTED IN POLAND

Prasowe Zakłady Graficzne RSW „Prasa-Książka-Ruch" — Wrocław,
ul. Piotra Skargi 3/5 — Cena zł 120,—